Being Ready:

A College Preparatory Resource for Third Culture Students

By Barbara J. Carter

Copyright © 2006 Barbara Jo Carter

All rights reserved. No portion of this book may be reproduced, stored in a retrieval system, or transmitted in any form or by any means, electronic, mechanical, photocopying, recording or otherwise without written permission of the author.

ISBN 978-1-60145-201-6
ISBN-10 1-60145-201-2

Leader's Guide to *Being Ready: A College Preparatory Resource* available from the author.

Contact:
Barbara J. Carter

being.ready.college.prep@gmail.com

Printed in the United States of America by:
©Booklocker.com
PO Box 2399
Bangor, ME 04402-2399

ACKNOWLEDGEMENTS

To my family, your love and encouragement have been my strength.

To my friends, your humor and companionship have kept me sane.

To my instructors, your wisdom and knowledge have challenged me.

To my fellow missionaries, your prayers and confidence have lifted me.

To my MKs, *han sido mi vida y mi pasión, gracias*.

To my God, You are everything to me, thank you.

In Loving Memory of Dr. Aulden Coble
1914-2006

"Blessed is the man who does not walk in the counsel of the wicked or stand in the way of sinners or sit in the seat of mockers. But his delight is in the law of the LORD, and on his law he meditates day and night. He is like a tree planted by streams of water, which yields its fruit in season and whose leaf does not wither. Whatever he does prospers."

Psalm 1:1-3

Table of Contents

Letter from the Author ix

Commitment Letter xi

Who Are You? xiii

Unit One: Our Relationship with God 1
   Day One: Where Did it All Begin? 2
   Day Two: What Does a Relationship with God Look Like? 5
   Day Three: Does a Relationship with God Really Matter? 8
   Day Four: Making It Real 12
   Day Five: Making It last 18

Unit Two: Our Relationship with Others 25
   Day One: God's Design 26
   Day Two: Loving Family 28
   Day Three: Loving Friends 32
   Day Four: Loving Others 34
   Day Five: Loving Well 37

Unit Three: Loving with the Heart – Emotional Preparation 41
   Day One: The "Heart" of the Bible 42
   Day Two: A "Heart" Exam 44
   Day Three: A "Heart" Exam 50
   Day Four: A "Heart" Exam 54
   Day Five: A Willing Heart 58

Unit Four: Loving with the Soul – Spiritual Preparation 61
   Day One: The "Soul" of the Bible 62
   Day Two: Priming our Souls 65
   Day Three: Growing from Others 67
   Day Four: Hearing from the Word 73
   Day Five: Biblical Basis for Life 81

Unit Five: Loving with Strength – Physical Preparation 83
   Day One: The "Body" of the Bible 84
   Day Two: Body 88
   Day Three: Body 94
   Day Four: Body 98
   Day Five: The Body and Stress 100

Unit Six: Loving with the Mind – Intellectual Preparation 109
   Day One: The "Mind" of the Bible 110

Day Two: Time Management 112
Day Three: Purposeful Reading 120
Day Four: Taking Note of Things 124
Day Five: Research and Writing 131

Unit Seven: Closing Thoughts 135

Summary Time 141

Class Evaluation 149

References 153

Letter from the Author

Dear "Soon-to-Be" College Student-

The Bible clearly illustrates for us God's laws. Deuteronomy instructs the Israelites to love God with all of their hearts, souls, and strength. In the book of Matthew, when questioned about the most important of the laws, Jesus answered in a similar way. "Love the Lord your God with all your heart and with all your soul and with all your mind" (Matt. 22:37). He also included a second law regarding relationship. "Love your neighbor as yourself" (Matt. 22:39). It is in these passages we discover the theology of relating to God and to others, as well, as the theology of the heart, the soul, the strength of mankind, and the mind.

My hope for the next several weeks is to outline the fundamental truths found in these passages. I believe that it will help prepare you for the transition to college not only on a practical level but as well on an emotional heart level, a spiritual soul level, strength of body level, a mind geared toward building the intellect, and a healthy relational level between you and God and you and others.

Let me encourage you to work through the assignments with the goal of learning from God and laying a solid foundation for college life, not with the goal of merely "filling in the blanks." Take the time needed to reflect on the assignments and discuss the topics with others. There are many resources out there to get you into college, but my desire is to not only see you "get in" but to excel relationally, emotionally, spiritually, physically, and intellectually. I fully believe that the ground work that you lay now, while in high school, will serve you well in college.

Transition to college is tough. For those of you who have grown up overseas the transition has added elements. Transition from your host countries to the United States for college is an extreme move. I believe that you, as young people especially those of you who are third culture kids, have a tremendous amount to offer those on the college campus, churches, ministries, and places of work. Basically, anywhere you land. I believe that any time you decide to live under the Lordship of Jesus and obey the laws of God, you will be blessed. I am firmly convinced that loving God with your heart, soul, strength, mind, and loving others will greatly assist in transitioning to college life.

Blessings in the Highest-

Dr. Barbara J. Carter (a.k.a. Miss B)

Commitment Letter

God has a great plan for your life. It is a plan for your highest good. The goal of this workbook is not just to help you be successful in college; it is to help you draw closer to God in your faith walk now. In order to help reach that goal it is important to complete the workbook and allow God to speak to you through the assignments. This will be easier accomplished if you are supported. I encourage you to find someone who can serve as your accountability partner. This could be a fellow classmate, a friend, a parent, a teacher whoever knows you well and will encourage you through the process.

I _____
(Please print your name)

commit to do my best to complete the workbook and allow God to speak to me through the assignments.

_____   _____
(Please sign your name)   (Date)

I _____
(Please print your accountability partner's name)

commit to do my best to pray for, encourage, and support _____ during this study.

_____   _____
(Please have your accountability partner sign here)   (Date)

_____
(Date completed)

Who Are You?

1. General Information:
   Name _____ Age _____ Grade _____

2. List the countries in which you have lived.
   _____
   _____
   _____
   _____
   _____

3. How many languages do you speak, read, and write?
   _____
   _____

4. Are your parents with a mission sending agency or supported by a church in another country (yes or no) if so which one?
   _____
   _____

5. How long have you lived where you are now?
   _____

6. What do you consider to be home?
   _____
   _____

7. What is your Father's nationality?
   _____

8. What is your Mother's nationality?
   _____

9. What is your biggest concern about going to college?
   _____
   _____

10. What do you most look forward to concerning college?
    _____
    _____

Unit One: Our Relationship with God

The Week at a Glance

†

Objectives

To see that it is God's design to have a relationship with each of us

To understand the importance of our relationship with God

To explore ways to enrich our relationship with God

†

Verse

"Love the Lord your God with all your heart, with all your soul, and with all your might."
-Deuteronomy 6:4

Our lives are filled with relationships. We bounce around on this planet bumping into others. In the bumping and bouncing we bond with and/or we repel others. This almost sounds like a science experiment with ions, protons, and electrons. We have varying relationships of varying degrees.

Some of our relationships are preprogrammed; family, for instance. Then there are some with whom we have a relationship created by circumstances that; co-workers, classmates, team members, neighbors, church members, or mission family. With some people we are automatically drawn to them, and although we've known them only a short while, we feel like we've known them all our lives. These are the kindred spirits and best friends in our lives.

It is true that all of life is made up of relationships. In this unit we are going to explore the most important relationship in the life of every human (whether they know it or not), and that is our relationship with the Creator of it all. We are going to look at the eternal importance of this relationship as well as how we can live it to the fullest.

Let's take time now to pray asking God to reveal Himself to us and make His Word come alive to us as we discover the meaning of a relationship with Him.

Day One: Where Did it All Begin?

The relationship between God and man began at creation (Gen. 1:26-2:25). The first Biblically recorded question to man came from the serpent, a question which planted seeds of doubt regarding the sincerity of God's spoken law (Gen. 3:1). The second Biblically recorded question came from God and was addressed to man (Gen. 3:9). This was not a question that was necessarily geographic in nature. God, being omnipresent, (Ps. 139) was privy to Adam and Eve's location. It was the rhetorical question, "Where are you?" (Gen. 3:9), which marked the Almighty's initial attempt to persuade mankind to understand the breech in their relationship with Him. This question seems to address the issue of relationship status. Where are they now in their relationship with God after the offense of disobedience? God has always desired a relationship with us, but because He is holy, He can not tolerate our sinful nature. When we sin we distance ourselves from God and cause a breech in our relationship with Him.[1] The question God asked Adam and Eve is the same for us today...

Where are we in our relationship with God?

Relationships are like stories. There is a point of introduction or beginning and a time of getting to know the other. Often there are ups and downs, moments of crisis shrouded with imminent danger, times of love, peace, and tranquility. Use the following space to tell the story of your relationship with God. You may just be beginning your story with Him. You might have known Him most of your life and would be able to write volumes. You might not have even opened the book yet. Express yourself! Remember to use good writing style.

_____
_____
_____
_____

---

[1] Ian F. Jones, "The Question and the Call, Chapel October 27, 2004." Fort Worth: Southwestern Baptist Theological Seminary, 2004. Speech.

A College Preparatory Resource for Third Culture Students

Being Ready

A College Preparatory Resource for Third Culture Students

Day Two: What Does a Relationship with God Look Like?

1. When you have a relationship with a person, say a friendship, how do you go about strengthening that relationship? Place a check by actions that occur when you build a friendship with someone.

☐ talk	☐ play	☐ celebrate	☐ hang out
☐ trust	☐ expect	☐ challenge	☐ listen
☐ pray	☐ express	☐ encourage	☐ give
☐ sacrifice	☐ love	☐ bless	☐ hugs
☐ advise	☐ console	☐ care	☐ believe
☐ defend	☐ support	☐ protect	☐ confide
☐ hope	☐ patient	☐ kind	☐ _____
☐ share	☐ dream	☐ chat (IM)	☐ _____
☐ correct	☐ tolerant	☐ worry	☐ _____
☐ have fun	☐ confront	☐ forgive	☐ _____
☐ guard	☐ help	☐ heal	☐ _____

2. From the list above, what seems to be the hardest and why?

_____

_____

_____

3. Do you see some of these elements in your relationship with God? Go back over the list and circle the items that are a part of your relationship with God.

4. Of the items not circled, what would you like to see developed in your relationship with God?

_____
_____
_____
_____
_____

Moses is a wonderful example of a simple man who had a friendship with God. Read the following passage aloud. Imagine yourself there as an undetectable observer. Picture the scenery, sense the smells, and feel the intimacy of this deep friendship between God and Moses.

The Tent of Meeting

[7] Now Moses used to take a tent and pitch it outside the camp some distance away, calling it the "tent of meeting." Anyone inquiring of the LORD would go to the tent of meeting outside the camp. [8] And whenever Moses went out to the tent, all the people rose and stood at the entrances to their tents, watching Moses until he entered the tent. [9] As Moses went into the tent, the pillar of cloud would come down and stay at the entrance, while the LORD spoke with Moses. [10] Whenever the people saw the pillar of cloud standing at the entrance to the tent, they all stood and worshiped each at the entrance to his tent. [11] The LORD would speak to Moses face to face, as a man speaks with his friend. Then Moses would return to the camp, but his young aide Joshua son of Nun did not leave the tent   -Exodus[2]

5. Go back and underline the parts of this passage that indicate the closeness of the relationship between God and Moses.

---

[2] Exod. 33:7-11, *Holy Bible, New International Version* (Nashville: Holman Bible Publishers, 1986). All Scriptures quoted are from this version of the Bible unless otherwise noted. Used by permission of Zondervan Bible Publishers.

6. What impressed you the most about this relationship and why?

_____
_____
_____
_____
_____

Moses was not a perfect person by any stretch of the imagination; however he was real with God and in his relationship to Him. Moses spent intimate time with God (Exod. 33:1-7), he trusted God to lead him (Exod. 3), he took his frustrations to God (Exod. 17:4), he listened and obeyed God (Exod. 17:6), he was touched by God (Exod. 33:12-23), etc. Moses was not a perfect man, but God the relationship perfect. The Lord of all creation wanted a relationship with His people, and He began through Moses.

Neither you nor I are perfect, however, the perfect God of the universe wants to befriend us. Just as any healthy relationship requires time and commitment, our relationship with God requires the same. The list that we first looked at today is only a beginning in building our relationship with God. A relationship with God necessitates daily effort. The last couple of days of this week we are going to look at practical ways in which we can build up our relationship with God.

The book of Ephesians epitomizes the relationship intentions of God for all of mankind. "For he chose us in him before the creation of the world to be holy and blameless in his sight. In love He predestined us to be adopted as His sons through Jesus Christ, in accordance with his pleasure and will to the praise of his glorious grace, which he has freely given us in the One he loves" (Eph. 1:4-6).

Day Three: Does a Relationship with God Really Matter?

We have seen over the last couple of days that it is God's plan to have a healthy relationship with each of us. We have also looked at what a relationship with God might resemble. Hopefully, you are beginning to view your relationship with God as something that is precious to Him. There is no doubt where God stands with us and what His point of view is concerning us. He loves us, treasures us, and wants to have a loving relationship with us.

God has clearly made His relationship intentions known to us through His written Word. It is God's kindness and patience that leads rebellious man to repentance (Rom. 2:4). Repentance is the desire of God for all humans. "He is patient with you, not wanting anyone to perish, but everyone to come to repentance" (2 Pet. 3:9b). God loves His creation of mankind and sacrificially took steps to bring us into a loving relationship with Himself (John 3:16). This relationship with the Almighty becomes possible through our repentance of sin and confession of Jesus Christ as the Son of God (Rom: 10:9-11).

Just think about it, with every sunrise since the dawn of time we have been on God's mind. He loves us deeply and desires for us to live in the shadow of the cross. Living in the shadow of the cross means that God sees us through His Son as holy and clean- forgiven. Remember that, although God wants us to live in a loving relationship with Him now and for eternity, He is still holy and we are not (not even close!). So how can a holy God live in a loving relationship with an unholy people? **Jesus**. He is our one word answer. The Bible tells us that all have sinned and fallen short of the glory of God (Rom. 3:23). Basically, God had the goal of us living lives of trust and obedience, lives of love and peace with Him, but as a whole we blew it.

The consequence of our choice to rebel against God was costly. "For the wages of sin is death" (Rom. 6:23). This is not just a physical death but a spiritual death and being our reality for all eternity. A spiritual death is simply separation from God and everything that is good. Because of what began in the Garden of Eden when Adam and Eve decided to disobey God (Gen. 3), we all have to pay the price of sin. The truth is that God was not taken by surprise when Adam and

Eve blew it nor is He taken back went we choose to sin against Him today. He had a plan for us even before we knew that we needed a plan; "God demonstrates His own love for us in this: While we were still sinners, Christ died for us" (Rom. 5:8). This is the really cool part; He did it because He loved us. We can't even come close to earning it; "He saved us, not because of righteous things we had done, but because of His mercy" (Titus 3:5). God wants to save us just because HE LOVES US! It's God's grace that makes it possible for you and me to come to Him - not our efforts. We can't earn it. It's a free gift. "For it is by grace you have been saved, through faith - and this not from yourselves, it is the gift of God - not by works, so that no one can boast" (Eph. 2:8-9).

1. Let's take a second to reflect on this complex thought. What do these above paragraphs say to you? Rewrite the main concepts in your own words.

_____
_____
_____
_____
_____
_____
_____
_____
_____

Jesus paid the price for your sins and mine by giving His life on the cross. God brought Jesus back from the dead and cleared the way for us to have a personal relationship with Him through Jesus. Now the "ball is in our court." It is our turn to respond to this amazing offer of love. We respond in only one of two ways, we can accept the gift that Jesus is holding out for us right now and live; "If you confess with your mouth, "Jesus is Lord," and believe in your heart that God raised him from the dead, you will be saved. For it is with your heart that you believe and are justified, and it is with your mouth that you confess and are saved" (Rom. 10:9-10), or we reject it and die. If we accept it, then our lives will begin a wonderful transformation (we'll talk more about this later). However, if we blow God off and reject His gift of life, our choice is death (the forever kind). God says that if you believe in His son, Jesus, you can live forever with Him in glory. "For God so loved the world that He gave his one and only Son, that whoever believes in him shall not perish, but have eternal life" (John 3:16).

2. How have you responded to God's offer of eternal life?

_____
_____
_____

3. If you have accepted Jesus Christ as Savior, how are you living your life differently than if you had not accepted His love? If not, why aren't you?

_____
_____
_____

4. If you are a believer but you are living your life to please yourself or someone else rather than God, then you won't see a change. If this is the case and you want to change, begin now. Take some time to pray asking God to be in charge of your life and then start living like He is.

5. Whether we believe in God and eternal life or not, that does not detract from the fact that what the Bible says about God is true. Whether we like it or not, we will all live eternally. Now where we take up permanent residence is our choice... the option is heaven or hell. You may have grown up on the mission field or gone to church all of your life, but if you have never really accepted Jesus as the Savior of your life and really are not sure where you will be spending eternity, then I strongly encourage you to stop now and talk with a Christian about accepting Christ as your personal Savior or pray now and then immediately share with someone the wonderful decision that you have made.

Here's a Suggested Prayer:

"Lord Jesus, I know that I am a sinner and I do not deserve eternal life. But, I believe You died and rose from the grave so that I would have a place in Heaven. Jesus, come into my life, take control of my life, forgive my sins and save me. I am trusting in You alone for my salvation, and I accept your free gift of eternal life."

God has an amazing and wonderful life of love planned for you. All He asks is that you love Him back. "However, as it is written; 'No eye has seen, no ear has heard, no mind has conceived what God has prepared for those who love him'" (1 Cor. 2:9).

Being Ready

Day Four: Making It Real

I have a couple of interesting statistics for you. Approximately three of every four teenagers in the United States of America consider themselves to be religious, most of them are following in the religious traditions and church affiliations of their parents. Despite the number of religious adolescents in North America, approximately eighty-eight percent of children raised in evangelical Christian homes leave church at age eighteen, never to return to church again.[3]

1. Why do you suppose so many say they are religious yet so many stop going to church once they get out of high school?

_____
_____
_____
_____
_____

High school graduates and college age people are emotionally ready to make serious commitments to Christ and are at the stage in life where they are taking purposeful steps toward career and even marriage. If college age students are not in church or actively pursuing a relationship with God, how will the generations to come know, love, and serve God with all their hearts, souls, and strength?

A relationship, by nature, must be maintained. We as Christians are not only in relationships with other believers; we are also in a relationship with the Most High. A relationship with God requires commitment and energy. We can't live on borrowed faith; our faith in God must be our own. If we are going to have a healthy relationship with God, we must make it real.

There are a number of spiritual disciplines (practices) that help us grow in our relationship with God. The discipline of solitude, meditation, silence, simplicity, discretion, sacrifice, fasting, submission, prayer, study, service, confession, worship, celebration, and fellowship are the

---

[3] Johnny Derouen, American Families in Crises Research. Class lecture for Human Growth and Development, [March 21, 2005]. Southwestern Baptist Theological Seminary, Ft. Worth, Texas.

areas that we will explore the next two days. Please know that the next two days will be a mere introduction to fifteen complex areas of study. My hope is that this will serve as a starting place for an exciting relationship.

The discipline of solitude: Solitude is the practice of being alone, absent from other people and other things so that we can be completely focused on being in the presence of God. When we practice the discipline of solitude, we stop planning, defending, analyzing, or making the world as we think it "should" be. We simply say to God in the stillness and the quiet; "Reveal Yourself to me, God. Show me all that You desire me to know about You and Your world around me." When and where can you begin regularly practicing the discipline of solitude?

_____

_____

_____

_____

The discipline of meditation: Someone once told me that if you have the ability to worry then you have the ability to meditate. There is some truth to this. Worry is nothing more than the turning and tossing a thought around in your mind like wet clothes being tossed in an industrial strength dryer. The big difference is that worry is when a thought has got a hold of you and meditation is when you get a hold of God's thoughts.

Meditation can occur anywhere, anytime. No special equipment required. When you read Scripture and the Holy Spirit reveals truth to you; think on it, study it, and look at it from all different angles. Ask God to show you the significance of His Word. Toss and turn that thought around until understanding is yours and that understanding changes the way you live. "Do not merely listen to the Word, and so deceive yourselves. Do what it says." James 1:22.

The discipline of silence: When I was little I played the "Quiet Game" with my brothers (mainly at times when I wanted them to stop bugging me). The "Quiet Game" is not exactly the same as the discipline of silence. Silence means to be quiet so that we can hear the voice of God. We have to stop talking (inner and outer voice) if we are to be able to listen to what God wants to say to us. In prayer we voice our thoughts to God but in silence we listen to His response, allowing Him to take as long as He needs to communicate to us. How many times, this week, have you sat in silence for the purpose of letting God speak to you? Make an appointment with God, in the next couple of days. Find a quiet place (not your bedroom, sleep doesn't qualify as silence). Don't put a time limit on this meeting. Sit in silence for as long as God needs you there. Write down some of the things about which He has spoke to you.

_____
_____
_____
_____
_____
_____

The discipline of simplicity: The practice of simplicity is getting rid of the aspiration for popularity, glamour, pleasure, and luxury. Don't hear me say that these things are evil in and of themselves. Simplicity has to do with our attitudes. Our attitude should be that these are added blessings in our lives that must produce praise, attributed to God. We are to invest in eternal things with all that God has given. Our attitude should not be to pursue them, realizing that these are not the things that make us have a fulfilled life. Simplicity is cutting back the extras in our lives, especially if they distract us from God. Evaluate the following items in your life.

Ask God to show you where you have excess and mark those items then ask Him what He wants you to do about them. The last step is to obey.

Item	What God wants me to do about it
☐ Money	_____
☐ Music	_____
☐ Sports	_____
☐ Clothes	_____
☐ Car	_____
☐ College	_____
☐ Entertainment	_____
☐ Hobby	_____
☐ Talent/gifts	_____
☐ Popularity	_____
☐ Intelligence	_____
☐ Skills/abilities	_____
☐ Electronics	_____
☐ _____	_____
☐ _____	_____

The discipline of discretion: Discretion is not just practicing good judgment, maturity, or tack. It is practicing a form of secrecy. Not running around as *incognito* Christians, in trench coats, dark sunglasses, and disguises. The discipline of discretion is doing acts of kindness without the goal of being recognized for it or doing it to get credit. When you practice this discipline, it is important that you do not lie or intentionally deceive others. Practicing the discipline of discretion is a response to God's love for us and His abundant blessings to us. This discipline reminds us that our value and identity does not come from the praise of others, but from the fact that God loves us. I encourage you to pray asking God what secret act of kindness He wants you to do today; be it a note of encouragement, giving some material item (food, clothes, money, etc.) to someone in need, unsolicited service... then do it. I don't even want you to report on it. That would take away from the whole idea of discretion.

The discipline of sacrifice: Sacrifice is a bit beyond simplicity. Simplicity is evaluating and giving up the "extras," whereas sacrifice is putting yourself in the place where you have to completely depend on God. Keep in mind that sacrifice is not financial, irresponsibility, or physical neglect. It is arranging your life in such a way that you have to completely trust in God. By nature college is a place where much sacrifice occurs for the sake of getting an education. The spiritual discipline of sacrifice is for others and will give you a deeper trust level in God. Find a Bible verse that will help you to remember to trust in God to meet all of your needs.

_____
_____
_____
_____
_____
_____
_____

The discipline of fasting: Fasting is not a dieting nor is it an attempt to force God to do something for us. It has the same purpose all other spiritual disciplines have and that is to focus our lives on God. With each hunger pang we are reminded to depend upon God for all things, to consider other's needs, and to have a grateful attitude for all that we do have. Begin slowly with this discipline once a month for a meal or two. Choose a passage or two of Scripture to meditate upon during your fast from food or drink. As you grow in this discipline, you will come to understand what Jesus meant when He said; "It is written: 'Man does not live on bread alone, but on every word that comes from the mouth of God'" (Matt. 4:4). Begin to practice this discipline by choosing one day and one meal from which to fast. Remember you are focusing on God and not yourself, so don't make a big deal out of your intentions by telling the whole world.

The discipline of submission: Submission is the spiritual discipline that helps us know that God is in control of every situation. When we submit to those who are in authority, we acknowledge the fact that God designed life with order and hierarchy. We are also trusting God's greater plan over our momentary circumstances and temporary situations. Not only are we to submit to earthly authorities but we are to pray for them, realizing that it is God who gives all authority. Above all powers on this earth our greatest act of submission is to the Will and Word of God. The practice of submission to earthly masters leads to being prepared to follow the leadership of God. List five authorities that you have in you life at this moment, praying for each, then list five possible authorities that you might have in college and pray for them as well.

1. _____

2. _____

3. _____

4. _____

5. _____

1. _____

2. _____

3. _____

4. _____

5. _____

Conclude the day's session in prayer asking God to help you know what areas of your relationship to Him need attention. Listen to Him and He will lead you. Remember He loves you deeply and desires this relationship with you. Focus your heart on Him.

Blessings!

Day Five: Making It last

Research indicates that the Christian rearing experienced in the home and church prior to university studies is **NOT** enough to sustain the spiritual growth in the life of a young believer. Church, once or twice a week, is not enough, chapel services at your school or mission are not enough, once a week dorm Bible study is not enough, going to the college praise and worship night once a week is not enough. We must be continually working on our relationship with God. We need to give attention to not only making it real but making it last. Today we are going to look at seven more spiritual disciplines that will help us increase the quality and the longevity of our relationship with God.

The discipline of prayer: Prayer is one of God's greatest favors to mankind. Just think about it, we don't have to carry a tabernacle around with us (Exod. 26), nor do we have to sacrifice animals or bring burnt offerings (Exod. 12:4-7) just to hold a conversation with God. Jesus surrendered beams of glory for hay in a stable. He traded the throne of supreme rule for the Roman cross. Because of Christ's sacrificial love for us, the temple veil was torn from top to bottom (Matt. 27:51) making a way for us to have access to God through direct personal prayer (Heb. 9). This is exciting stuff! Anywhere, anytime… He is there to hear our heart's cry. Prayer is a continual conversation with God. There are prayers of thanksgiving, of repentance, of petition, of praise, of sorrow, and of intersession – all of them conversations. Some people write their prayers in a journal, some sing them, some pray the Scriptures, some pray aloud, some with accountability partners, and some pray liturgies. Regardless of the method and regardless of the style, prayer must be a constant in our lives. How can we hope to have any type of relationship without communication?

Write out two methods of prayer, share your ideas with your accountability partner or someone else and then choose one of these ideas to practice for the weekend.

A College Preparatory Resource for Third Culture Students

PRAYER

1.

___

2.

___

The discipline of study: "All Scripture is God-breathed and is useful for teaching, rebuking, correcting and training in righteousness, so that the man of God may be thoroughly equipped for every good work" (2 Tim. 3:16). Paul writes in his letter to Timothy exactly what the Bible is and why we have it. Write the above passage in your own words, defining the Bible.

___

Being Ready

If the Bible is a key to our understanding of God and His plan for us, don't you think that it is pretty important? When the Israelites were trekking through the wilderness on their forty year hiking trip, God provided daily manna for them (literally bread from heaven). The deal was that they had to gather only what they needed to survive for that day. They couldn't store up manna and have leftovers because they needed a fresh batch each day (Exod.16). The Bible is daily bread for us (Matt. 4:4). We can't survive on Scriptural leftovers from Sunday's sermon. We need a fresh word from God each day. There are so many approaches to Bible study; reading through the Bible in a year, topical Bible studies, inductive Bible studies, devotional readings based on and including Scripture, group Bible studies, on-line studies…the list goes on. We will look some more at these different practical methods of Bible study in unit four. The point here is that Bible study is a major spiritual discipline one that must be practiced daily for a healthy long-term relationship with God. Find something that works for you. Don't just study it, memorize it, then live it.

*"Do not merely listen to the Word, and so deceive yourselves. **Do what it says**. Anyone who listens to the Word but does not do what it says is like a man, who looks at his face in a mirror and, after looking at himself, goes away and immediately forgets what he looks like. But the man who looks intently into the perfect law that gives freedom, and **continues to do this**, not forgetting what he has heard, **but doing it** – he will be blessed in what he does."*
-James 1:22-25

The discipline of service: When we practice the discipline of service, we are putting the needs of others before ours and in our agendas. The way that service draws us nearer to God is that we resign the need for control in our hearts and take on the heart of a giver. In serving others, we find our true identities in God not in who we are or what we've accomplished for ourselves. Jesus set the example for us to follow.

1. Read John 13:1-17 and answer the following.
2. What is important about verse 3 and Jesus' identity?

_____

_____

3. What is significant about the task of washing feet?

_____

_____

4. What was the teaching point that Jesus was trying to communicate?

The discipline of confession: The spiritual discipline of confession is a hard one for us to practice because none of us like to admit it when we mess up. Even though it is difficult, confession is a necessary part of maintaining a healthy relationship with God. If we sin (wait, not if…but when we sin), we need to go directly to God and ask for His forgiveness. The Bible tells us that if we confess our sins that God is faithful and just to forgive us of our sins and to cleans us from all unrighteousness (1 John 1:9). The Bible also outlines a safeguard for us. Within the body of Christ there is to be accountability to each other. We are to help one another on this Christian trek. Confession is purely a trust based practice. "Therefore, confess your sins to each other and pray for each other so that you may be healed. The prayer of a righteous man is powerful and effective" (Jas. 5:16). Why it is important to confess our sins to each other?

How important do you think it is to seriously pray for each other where sin is concerned? Why?

The discipline of worship: Giving glory, praise, honor, and worth-ship to God. Worship is making it all about Him. Far too often people confuse worship with going to church or as a style of music. Worship is saying or doing **anything** with the intention of exulting God. "So whether you eat or drink or whatever you do, do it all for the glory of God" (1 Cor. 10:31). You can wash dishes with the intention of worshipping God. "Whatever you do, work at it with all your heart, as working for the Lord, not men" (Col. 3:23). Worship is an attitude of the heart. It is a disposition that you decide to take on at the beginning of the day. Attitudes of worship throughout our lifetime will draw us close to God and keep us there. It is a simple change of our world view. It is seeing God in everything from the sunrise, to the sunset, from the flower to the great canyon, from the face of a newborn to the crippled body of the aged, and from the times of peace to the times of war. Worship is a heart of gratitude that continually gives the credit back to the Creator and King.

We can worship God in the daily routine of our lives by our attitudes, but we also set aside unique times of special focus on God (chapel, church, devotional times). Design a special appointment of worship. Think in terms of a group time of devotional, a chapel service, a family devotional, or a class time of worship. You are worshipping the author of creativity. BE CREATIVE!!!

The discipline of celebration: As believers and as young people we have much to celebrate. Faith in Christ Jesus brings us into a whole new family dynamic with new family traditions of celebration. The Israelites were among the first to establish the spiritual discipline of celebration. Celebration is a form of worship. In simple terms, it is remembering what God has done and with a heart of gratitude, celebrating His goodness and worthiness. Celebration is also acknowledging the victory that lies ahead for all those belonging to God. Paul said; "I have fought the good fight, I have finished the race, I have kept the faith" (2 Tim. 4:7). While on this planet we are in a good fight for faith, and we are running the race of becoming like Christ. Victory is ours, and we celebrate it!

The discipline of fellowship: Remember the statistic that I gave you yesterday concerning kids who grow up in church leaving church once they get to college? One of the reasons they stop going to church is that they don't practice the spiritual discipline of fellowship. Hebrews says; "Let us not give up meeting together, as some are in the habit of doing, but let us encourage one another - and all the more as you see the Day approaching" (Heb. 10:25). Our purpose for getting together is to encourage one another. College is tough enough for anyone, especially MKs, we can't do life alone. Now is not the time to stop hanging out with other believers. For those of you who are MKs and TCKs it is highly likely that church in the United States will be very different than anything that you have ever experienced. Many of you have been an active part of ministry on the field, starting churches, leading Bible studies, or openly evangelizing in your neighborhoods and school. Some of you have attended church is someone's house all your life, or in a warehouse, a barn, a place of business, or underneath a mango tree.

Many churches in the US can be overwhelming the first time you visit. The building size, the number of people, and the general socio-economic background of the members may send you reeling emotionally. But don't be overcome by it. It is normal to have feelings of anger, sadness, home-sickness, frustration, and self –righteousness. Again, don't be overcome by it. Experience the feelings yet do not sin. Look at this as an opportunity to see how others worship and celebrate their faith. Ask God to help you find a core group of believers with whom you can grow. Even if you don't find a church "home" until your second semester, senior year – keep looking. Remember that it is not all about you. Other believers need your fellowship as well. They need your daily encouragement as the book of Hebrews describes.

College ministries are another wonderful place to experience and exercise the spiritual discipline of fellowship. Many universities have organizations such as The Fellowship of Christian Athletes (heads up on this one…you don't have to be an athlete to participate), Baptist Student Ministry, Campus Crusade, Christian Fellowship, etc. Dorm Bible studies, campus devotional groups Christian club fellowships, and churches with college ministries are great sources of fellowship. The point here is that fellowship is an important spiritual discipline designed to help us maintain a long-term relationship with God.

Unit Two: Our Relationship with Others

> **The Week at a Glance**
>
> ✝
>
> **Objectives**
>
> To see God's relationship design for us
>
> To understand the important relationships in our lives
>
> To explore ways to enrich our relationships with others
>
> ✝
>
> **Verse**
>
> "Love the Lord your God with all your heart, with all your soul, and with all your mind. This is the first and greatest commandment, the second is like it: Love you neighbor as yourself. All the Law and the Prophets hang on these two commandments"
>
> -Matthew 22:37-40

Henri Nouwen once said; "The mystery of ministry is that we have been chosen to make our own limited and very conditional love the gateway for the unlimited and unconditional love of God." Because we have been so completely loved by God, through Jesus Christ, we ought to love each other (1 John 4:14). It is only through Jesus that man can love as Jesus loved, both God and man (Phil. 4:13). Wow, loving God is one thing, but loving others is another... we are all so... human!

Jesus was asked what was the most important of the laws. He answered the opposition with the Word of God (Deut. 6:4-5). Jesus' purpose was to do the will of his Father (John 5:30). Jesus identified himself in word, in deed, and in relationship with the Father (John 10:30). He responded by saying that our love for God is to be above all other laws, then we are to love others (Matt. 22:37). The love of neighbor has as its source, pattern, and concluding principle the love of God. We are going to look at God's design for the body of Christ, important relationships, and how we love God by loving others.

Day One: God's Design

No Man is an Island

...no man is an island, entire of itself;

every man is a piece of the continent, a part of the main.

If a clod be washed away by the sea, Europe is the less,

.... any man's death diminishes me,

for I am involved in mankind,

And therefore never send to know for whom the bell tolls;

It tolls for thee.

-John Donne

Several years ago Hollywood produced a movie about a stranded cast away. The protagonist was a top employee of a major company. He was driven by time, work, and control over his world. Although he was surrounded by people, he was alone, even the relationship with his girlfriend was distant and lacking serious commitment. His predicament worsened when his flight from the eastern hemisphere crashes, and he is left marooned on a deserted island.

On the island he finds his pager destroyed by water. This is symbolic of him loosing a sense of control over his world. This survivor's disconnectedness from mankind is exemplified in the shallow eulogy he speaks over a dead flight member. The solitude of the island provides him with an opportunity to reflect on and come to terms with the emptiness of his previous life. He even resorts to befriending a volleyball that he finds floating in the wreckage. God has designed us for community and relationship with one another. As the writer John Donne so perfectly puts it;

"No man is an island."

A College Preparatory Resource for Third Culture Students

Take a look at I Corinthians 12:12-31. What can we learn about God's plan for relationship through this passage? The body is a perfect analogy for God's relationship design. Answer the following questions and cite the verses that support your responses.

1. In the body of Christ are we all alike and do we have the same job?
   _____

2. Can we live the Christian life without each other?
   _____

3. What binds us all together?
   _____
   _____

4. What are some of the specific roles that members of the body might have?
   _____
   _____
   _____

5. How does the rest of the body respond when something is going on with one part or the other (hint: verses 25 and 26)?
   _____
   _____
   _____

It is God's plan for every believer to build relationships with other believers. We can't do life on our own (at least not very well). As children of God, we have the world and the prince of this world against us. The last thing that we need to do is try to live in the world as if we were the only ones here (we might just end up talking to volleyballs). We need a relationship with each other that is built on love, and in doing this we are living testimonies of Jesus Christ. Jesus said; "A new command I give you: Love one another. As I have loved you, so you must love one another. By this all men will know that you are my disciples, if you love one another" (John 13:34-35).

Day Two: Loving Family

When you think about the most influential people in your life, who are the first five people that come to mind? Most people include parents in their list, and with good reason. It is the divine plan of God that parents be the first and most influential spiritual teachers in the lives of their children. An extensive survey and interview project, by the National Study of Youth and Religion, conducted on the campus of the University of North Carolina at Chapel Hill, 2001-2005, statistically affirms the significance of Deuteronomy 6:4-7. Dr. Christian Smith along with the contribution of Melinda Lundquist Denton discovered that parents are the most important social influence on the spiritual lives of their teenagers. The religious life that parents model, to a large extent directly impacts and shapes the religious understanding and habits of their adolescent sons and daughters.[4] Parents have a pretty huge job of making sure you have everything you need to be God loving people when you grow up. Be sure that you thank them today for all they do in your life to help you become adults. Don't wait until you are in college and homesick (with dirty clothes piled in the corner of your dorm room, no gasoline in your car, sick of eating cafeteria food, and tired of your roommate's snoring) to appreciate what your parents do for you.

Parents are important, but don't forget your siblings and other relatives that you leave behind when you head off to college. Family is a major key to who we are and how we view the world. Family is important to us no matter how old we are or how independent we become. No matter how far away you are from family, there is a connectedness that spans continents. You, MKs and kids of expatriates, are amazing people. You have often been described as not being of your parent's home culture or completely of your families host culture. You are not even a combination of the two; rather you have created an entirely new reality called the third culture. Because "home" doesn't necessarily mean one country or another, family may become home to you. I once asked a student; "Where is home?" and they responded; "In whatever country mom and dad are this month." With the possibility that "home" may be in another country, aren't you thankful for the internet and for advances made with the telephone? **Stay connected**, you still

---

[4]Christian Smith, *Soul Searching: The Religious and Spiritual Lives of American Teenagers* (New York: Oxford University Press, 2005), 56.

need them even though you are half a world away, across the country, or on the other side of town.

"Children, obey your parents in the Lord, for this is right. 'Honor your father and mother' – which is the first commandment with a promise – 'that it may go well with you and that you may enjoy long life on the earth'" (Eph. 6:1-3). What better way to honor your parents than by including them in your assignment. Set up a time with your mom or dad (both if possible). Invite them out for a meal or a cup of coffee to meet with you, or make dinner for them. The point is, make it special. Tell them that you want to ask them some important questions. It might help them to know that you are doing an assignment. Parents are usually very interested in you doing well on homework assignments and if you haven't ask them for help since grade school (after the shock), they might be overjoyed that you asked them for help on your homework. Once you have their undivided attention, ask them the questions on the following page. Be sure that you listen to them completely before you summarize their responses in writing. Listen, don't debate…just listen.

1. Tell me what it was like the day I was born?

_____
_____
_____
_____
_____
_____
_____
_____
_____
_____
_____
_____
_____

2. When I was a little kid, did you ever worry about me? If so what concerned you?

3. When have you been the most proud of me?

4. What are some of your hopes and dreams for me?

_____
_____
_____
_____
_____
_____
_____
_____
_____
_____
_____
_____

5. When I go off to college what will you miss the most about me?

_____
_____
_____
_____
_____
_____
_____
_____
_____
_____
_____
_____

…turning the hearts of the fathers back to their children.

-Luke 1:17

Day Three: Loving Friends

Over the years social theorists have found that instruction has a role in socialization; however, it is believed that motivations and attitudes are basically "caught" from those who have strongly influenced us or with whom we have a strong emotional bond. At the Passover Feast, Jesus gathered with his disciples and close followers for the celebration. After the evening meal, he stepped away from the table and began to wash their feet. At the conclusion of this unprecedented event Jesus said; "Now that I, your Lord and Teacher, have washed your feet, you also should wash one another's feet. I have set an example that you should do as I have done for you" (John 13:14-15). Close friends deeply impact us and influence our behavior. I've heard my mom say that if I wanted to know what kind of person I am all I have to do is look at my friends. Jesus loved his close followers and disciples; "I no longer call you servants' because a servant does not know his master's business. Instead, I have called you friends, for everything that I learned from my Father I have made known to you" (John 15:15).

"My command is this: Love each other as I have loved you. Greater love has no man than this that he lay down his life for his friends. You are my friends if you do what I command" (John15:13-14). Christ exemplified this passage on the cross right after that last Passover supper with His friends. Jesus' influence on his friends was powerful. They left their homes and livelihoods to learn from him. They worked without pay and literally gave their lives because of their friend, Jesus. How do your friends influence you? How do you influence your friends?

College can be a wonderful time in your life; new places, new experiences, and new people. It is fundamentally important that you know who you are and who you want to be before going into this new world. No, I don't mean that you have to have the answers to all of life's questions and know exactly what you will major in. In choosing who you will befriend during your college years, an internal compass guiding who you are, is essential. Remember friends influence friends. Choose carefully who you hang with, study with, and go out with. Find other Christians who will challenge you and encourage you. Don't get yourself into relationships that constantly draw you away from God, but rather befriend people who make you desire God more. Take stock of your present friendships.

A College Preparatory Resource for Third Culture Students

1. With whom do you spend most of your time?
   _____

2. Who has the most influence in your relationship? Give an example.
   _____
   _____
   _____
   _____

3. How often do you and your friend talk about spiritual things?
   ☐ never ☐ every once in a while ☐ once a week ☐ everyday

4. How often do you pray with your friend?
   ☐ never ☐ every once in a while ☐ once a week ☐ everyday

5. How often to you read, study, or discuss the Bible together?
   ☐ never ☐ every once in a while ☐ once a week ☐ everyday

6. Does this friendship draw you closer to God? Why or why not?
   _____
   _____
   _____
   _____
   _____

7. If you answered no, are you willing to give the friendship over to God?
   _____
   _____
   _____
   _____
   _____
   _____
   _____

Being Ready

Day Four: Loving Others

We talked about two of the most important areas of relationships; family and friends. Today's topic is huge…loving everybody else! For believers, this category can break down into two parts; those who are Christians and those who are not. Within these two divisions, Scripture can show us how to view our neighbor, government authorities, our employers, our employees, college roommates, professors, the Dean of Students, and anyone else we might come across. Let's first take a look at what the Bible says concerning our behavior towards those who are not Christians.

Look up the following passages of Scripture that speak to how first century Christians should treat non-Christians and reflect on the meaning regarding our topic. Write down the basic principles that the Bible is teaching and how the principles apply to Christ-followers of the twenty-first century.

1. **Colossians 4:5**

   _____
   _____
   _____
   _____

2. **1 Thessalonians 4:11-12**

   _____
   _____
   _____
   _____

3. **2 Corinthians 6:14**

   _____
   _____
   _____
   _____

These passages tell us that we should set a godly example for others by living lives that are quiet, hard working, peaceable, engaging, and of a good reputation. We need to have good relationships with non-believers, but they are to be purposeful relationships. We are never to compromise who we are or the God we represent, but we are to try to identify with all sorts of folks that we might win them for the sake of Christ (1 Cor. 9:1-9). Never be deceptive about your relationship intentions with people. Your sincerity and honesty will bear greater witness to the love of Christ than manipulation or deceit.

> **Let your conversations be full of Grace and focused on Christ**

There are many more passages of Scripture pertaining to how Christians should treat one another. Instead of looking up all of those passages, let's read two chapters that summarize how we should consider one another in the body of Christ.

Read 1 John 2–3 and outline the principles by which Christians should live.

_____
_____
_____
_____
_____
_____
_____
_____
_____
_____
_____

Being Ready

A College Preparatory Resource for Third Culture Students

Day Five: Loving Well

One of the most influential characteristics of the Redeemer is His relentless compassion. Jesus was compassionate for the masses who were lost like sheep without a shepherd (Matt. 9:35-36). He was equally compassionate for His family (John 19:27) and His friends (John 11:33-36). The writer of James said of Jesus; "The Lord is full of compassion and mercy" (James 5:11). Compassion is the example that Christ modeled for his followers and the example that we are to follow now. "Be kind and compassionate to one another, forgiving each other, just as in Christ God forgave you" (Eph. 4:32). Jesus loved all people.

This week we have looked at God's perfect relationship design, the significance of loving family, the importance of loving friends, and the value of loving others; believers and non-believers alike. Today we are going to put our compassion in practice by looking at some practical ways of maintaining our important relationships.

One of the toughest things about going to college is saying good bye. You have taken years to build important relationships in your family, at school, in your mission, with church members, and with friends. It would be a shame to lose these treasured people due to communication neglect. As we discovered in the first week, relationships require our attention and care.

1. Other than your family, what five people or groups of people will you miss most when you leave for college?

   _____
   _____
   _____
   _____
   _____

2. Are these relationships worth the extra effort required to maintain them?

   _____
   _____

Being Ready

3. Are any of the following items possible to do:
   - Pray for your friends on a continual basis
   - Write letters, e-mails, or instant message them on a frequent basis
   - Call them (Voice Over Inter-net Protocol is a great option)
   - Holiday visits, summer vacations, or weekends

   - _____
   - _____

4. Another important thing to do before leaving for college is "say what needs to be said." I don't mean unloading all the negative things you can think of, about the person, that have driven you crazy over the years. Don't list all the bad habits and idiosyncrasies that the person has. If you need to ask for forgiveness, do it. If you need to clear the air about an unsettled issue or mistake, do it. Equally as important, you need to be sure to let people know how special they are to you and how much you appreciate them. Don't wait until you see them at your high school graduation to tell them how much they mean to you. Start now!

5. Is there anyone with whom you have an unsettled issue? _____

6. If so, go now to take care of business. Don't wait settle it (Matt. 5:23).

7. In reference to the five people you listed in question number one, make a list of at least three edifying things that you want to say to them, perhaps special things they have done for you, ways they have encouraged you, things they have taught you, positive characteristics in their life that you want to have in your own, etc. Once you have made the list, go and communicate these items to them. Remember don't wait, do it now. By the way, you are not limited to only five people or only three items for each. This is to just get you started.

First person:

_____
_____
_____

Second person:

_____
_____
_____

Third person:

_____
_____
_____

Forth person:

_____
_____
_____

Fifth person:

_____
_____
_____

Another person:

_____
_____
_____

Another person:

_____
_____
_____

"A word aptly spoken is like apples of gold in settings of silver."

-Proverbs 25:11

8. Don't "burn your bridges!" Most of you are hoping that as soon as that diploma is in your hand, you are jumping on a plane, a bus, a donkey or some other form of transportation…never to look back. This might be the case; however, it is vitally important to maintain good relationships with those you leave behind. You never know when you will need a letter of recommendation, transcript, word of wisdom, a place to stay while revisiting your country etc. I'm not telling you that …it's all about you! Maintaining good relationships with people because it benefits you, should not be your only motivation.

9. Remember that, with time, relationships change. Don't expect that things will be the same when you return from college or meet up with high school friends down the road. Know that this change is a normal part of life. Treasure the friendships and memories from high school and embrace the new challenges of college and the new relationships that will come your way.

10. In this time of transition remember that there is a friend who sticks closer than a brother (Pr. 18:4). God will never leave you nor forsake you (Jos. 1:5). When all these changes in relationships come, open your heart to Him (Ps.46). Remember you are not walking this journey alone (Matt. 28:20).

The Week at a Glance

†

Objectives

To see how the Bible views the human heart

To understand the significance of examining our hearts; sins, motives, and emotions

To explore ways to make the emotional adjustment to college

†

Verse

"And this is love: that we walk in obedience to his commands. As you have heard from the beginning, his command is that you walk in love.

-2 John 1:6

Unit Three:

Loving with the Heart –

Emotional Preparation

Broken-heartedness is seen in many areas of society. One of the most devastating evidences of this hopelessness is suicide. Regardless of age, sex or race, suicide is a leading cause of death for all persons, in the US. It is one of the top three reasons why young people aged 15 to 24, die every year. Depression, during the college years, is a common result of stress caused by: greater academic challenges, financial demands, new environment, change in family dynamics, and change in social life, exposure to new cultures, new temptations, and the pressures of life after graduation. "The transition from high school to college appears to be as hard on students' self-concepts (popularity, popularity with the opposite sex, leadership ability, social self-confidence, understanding of others, and the like) as it is on their academic self-images."[5] Transition to college life can be tough on the heart. This week we will look at being emotionally prepared for college.

---

[5] Ernest T. Pascarella, and Patrick T. Terenzini, *How College Affects Students,* (San Pascarella, Francisco: Jossey-Bass Publishers, 1991), 174.

Day One: The "Heart" of the Bible

What does the Bible have to say about the human heart? Strong's concordance of the Bible translates the word "heart" found in Deuteronomy as being the seat of emotions and passions, inclinations, resolution, determination of the will, reflection, and understanding.[6]

The Bible tells us that God searches the hearts of men and knows their motives (1 Chron. 28:9). The psalmist asked God for an undivided heart of devotion to his Creator (Ps. 86:11). The sinfulness of man is closely associated with the status of his heart; the heart is a seed-bed of sin (Gen. 6:5), it is wicked (Jer. 17:9), and it is perverse (Prov.11:20). Despite its corrupt state, the heart of man is the center of God's redemptive focus (Matt. 1:21, Luke 19:10). God requires of man an earnestness in seeking the restoration of his heart (Deut. 4:29). Man is to set his heart on things not of this earth, but rather of heaven and on the things of God (Col. 3:1).

The heart is precious and is the instrument by which God requires devotion; therefore, it must be protected (Prov. 4:23). The heart of man is revealing of a man's inner thoughts and motives (Matt. 12:34), including what he regards as valuable (Matt. 6:21). God desires our whole expression of love (Deut. 6:4-5). The psalmist pleads to God for an examination of the heart that God might lead him in the path of the everlasting (Ps. 139:1, 23-24). King David, a man after God's own heart (1 Sam. 13-14), asks for a pure and clean heart (Ps. 51:10) so that he might honor the name of God all the days of his life. Emotional preparedness, heart examination, and complete devotion is the start of peace with God (1 John 3:20).

Wow! The Bible has a lot to say about the heart of man and human emotions. It is obvious that our hearts are of great interest to God. We have just been bombarded with lots of information concerning our hearts. Let's review.

---

[6] James Strong, *The New Strong's Expanded Exhaustive Concordance of the Bible,* "heart," (Nashville: Thomas Nelson Publishers, 2001), 139.

A College Preparatory Resource for Third Culture Students

1. Who is the only one who can read the motives of man's heart? _____

2. What kind of devotion does the Creator want from man? _____

3. Where does sin begin? _____

4. What does God want to do with the human heart? _____

5. On what should man set his heart's attention?
_____

6. The heart reveals what about man? _____

7. What is the starting place to complete peace with God?
_____

8. What is it about our heart that concerns God most?
_____
_____
_____

9. Why would it be so important to constantly examine your heart or motives?
_____
_____
_____

10. Why do you suppose it is so important to guard your emotions? Is that the same thing as hiding your emotions? What is the difference?
_____
_____
_____
_____
_____

Today's assignment is to pray as the Psalmist did. Read Psalm 139 as a prayer to God; read it several times. Ask Him to examine your heart and show you what drive you. If anything is offensive, confess it and change direction.

Day Two: A "Heart" Exam

I have a friend, in Costa Rica, who is a cardiologist. One day I took my Biology class on a field trip to her office and to the hospital where she works. As we were walking through the area where she and her colleagues perform open heart surgery, I noticed several long tubes encased in plastic, hanging on the wall. When I asked her about them, she said that they were used to transport a camera up through a person's veins in their legs in order to examine their heart. The procedure is called cardiac catheterization. OUCH!!!

She said that she must do a careful examination of the heart in order to diagnose the person correctly, often saving their lives. She said; "If I miss even the smallest thing, the patient could die." You and I need cardiac catheterization, in a spiritual sense!

The passage that we looked at yesterday, Psalm 139 begins and ends with a heart exam. "O Lord, you have searched me and you know me...Search me, O God, and know my heart; test me and know my anxious thoughts" (Ps. 139:1, 23). Just as a cardiologist must do a careful examination of the physical heart, we must lay our hearts open before the Great Physician. It is a matter of eternal life or death; "For it is with your heart that you believe and are justified, and it is with your mouth that you confess and are saved" (Rom. 10:10).

Heart examination is vital for our eternal well-being. However, there is no question, that heart examination is also needed to help us live the full abundant life that Jesus came to give (John 10:10). Emotional well being begins and ends with complete honesty. In a heart exam you can't hide things. Just like in a cardiac catheterization, the heart must be carefully examined. This is not easy. No one likes for their sins to be identified, their wrong motivations to be revealed, or their guarded emotions to be exposed. Over the next few days we are going to look at three items that deeply affect our hearts; sins, motives, and emotions. I encourage you to be open and honest and allow God to work in your heart knowing that He loves you and cares deeply for you (1 John 3:1).

Sin... the Number One Cause of Spiritual Heart Disease

*"As a prisoner for the Lord, then, I urge you to **live a life worthy** of the calling you have received. Be completely **humble** and **gentle**; be **patient, bearing** with one another in love. Make every effort to keep the unity of the Spirit through the bond of peace. There is one body and one Spirit- just as you were called to one hope when you were called- one Lord, one faith, one baptism; one God and Father of all, who is over all and through all and in all."*

-Ephesians 4:1-6

God has a high calling for those that are His own. This calling requires all that we have as believers, every ounce of ourselves to be dedicated to our Lord and King. There is no room in our lives for the excess baggage of sin. There are a number of ways to review our hearts for sin. We are going to take a look at the heart by taking inventory based on the Ephesians 4:1-6 passage.

"Living worthy"

1. How often do you spend time in personal (just you and God) Bible study, prayer, and worship?

___ Everyday (sometimes twice a day), very consistent and strong

___ About 3 to 4 times a week, fairly consistent

___ Once a week…maybe, I only do it when someone reminds me

___ Used to, but I don't now

___ Only when I am in a Bible study group and I have to do the homework

___ Never have had a set aside time for a personal quiet time

2. If you are having a set aside time with God or had in the past, did you follow a program or study? If so, what worked best for you?

_____
_____
_____
_____
_____
_____

Being Ready

3. Are you open to begin today, meeting with Jesus. If not, what is holding you back?

_____
_____
_____

4. If Jesus physically walked the planet again and decided to hang out with you; with what books, magazines, DVDs, CDs, games, movies, TV programs, music, etc. would He be uncomfortable with in your life?

_____
_____
_____

5. Can others tell that you are a Christ follower? If so what evidence would they base it on?

_____
_____
_____
_____

6. Are you ever embarrassed to tell others that you are a Christian? Are there people with whom you refuse to talk about spiritual things? If so, why?

_____
_____
_____
_____

7. What would you be willing do to "live" for Jesus?

_____
_____
_____
_____

"Being completely humble"

8. What does Christian humility mean to you?

_____
_____
_____
_____
_____
_____
_____
_____

9. A former teacher of mine once defined Christian humility as seeing oneself as God does; no greater, no less. Does this definition sound like you? Do you see yourself as God sees you, no false sense of humility (using "self-demeaning" comments or behavior), or no false sense of pride (believing that you are better than or more important than other or even believing that you don't need God).

_____
_____
_____
_____

10. What are some of your natural abilities? (i.e. music, sports, art, organization)

_____
_____
_____
_____
_____
_____
_____
_____

11. Go back and underline all the ones that you want to do better, for the glory of God. As you underline them, ask God to help you turn those talents over to Him so that He can make them perfect for His purpose.

"Being completely gentle"

12. Generally speaking; how do you treat others?

_____
_____
_____
_____

13. Are your words always kind, encouraging, and edifying to those around you; even your siblings? _____

14. When was the last time that you committed a random act of kindness? How about doing something today? Give it a try, be creative.

"Being patient"

15. Being patient is extending to another person grace and mercy, even when they don't ask for it or know that they need it. Being patient is giving time, energy, tolerance, and love to someone, especially when they don't deserve it. With whom do you need to be more patient?

_____
_____
_____
_____

"Bearing with others"

16. I once walked along the Atlantic coast on my way to the port city of Limon, in Costa Rica. I stopped to ask how much further I had to go. The salty old Caribbean fisherman responded; "It depends, my love." Thinking that the tide, or wind, or land formation, in some odd way, had something to do with the distance I asked; "Depends on what?" He replied with a toothless grin;

"Are you walking alone or are you walking with a friend? It is always a shorter distance with a friend." What wisdom in that old man's words.

People are a gift. Friends and family are to be treasured. But that treasure can often seem like a burden. This is where the instruction to "bear" with each other comes in. None of us are perfect and all of us need others to put up with us from time to time. I think this is why the Bible says so many times to love each other. He knew that we needed a little slack with our idiosyncrasies, attitudes, mood swings, mistakes, the list goes on. What are some of the things that you hope your future roommate, classmates, professors, etc. will "bear" with you in?

_____
_____
_____
_____
_____
_____
_____
_____
_____

What are some things that you find hard to "put up with" in others?

_____
_____
_____
_____
_____
_____
_____
_____
_____

Bring these things before the Lord. Ask Him to help you see other as He does. Ask Him to help you bear with those He has placed in your life.

Day Three: A "Heart" Exam

Motives...What moves us and why

Why do we do the things we do? This seems to be a pretty important question since the motives of our hearts will come to light at the return of Jesus Christ: "Therefore judge nothing before the appointed time; wait till the Lord comes. He will bring to light what is hidden in darkness and will expose the motives of men's hearts. At that time each will receive his praise from God (1 Cor 4:5).

There are many things that may motivate us at any given time. Serious hunger may motivate us to eat chocolate wrapped in tortillas (or maybe that is just me). Fear of failing a Bible test may motivate us to stay up all night long, cramming class notes of the prison epistles into our tired minds. Interest in a special person may motivate us to do all kinds of crazy things. It is a good idea to understand where motives come from because our hearts can be easily deceived. "All a man's ways seem innocent to him, but motives are weighed by the LORD" (Prov. 16:2).

We are going to take a look at two major theories concerning motives. The drive theory and the arousal theory each have a lot to do with physical (biological) influences. The drive theory says that all humans have basic needs that must be met, things such as hunger, thirst, safety, acceptance, importance etc. Psychologists believe that all of our motivations come from an attempt to meet these basic needs, at their varying levels. The arousal approach is similar in that we attempt to meet our basic needs. However, arousal theorists believe that the level of satisfaction changes over a period of time depending on our experiences and our situations. These folks believe that we try to keep a balance physically by maintaining what they call *homeostasis.* The motive to meet our basic physical, social, psychological, and spiritual needs are normal and a part of God's design. However the way in which we meet those needs is crucial.

The Bible tells us that; "His divine power has given us everything we need for life and godliness through our knowledge of him who called us by his own glory and goodness" (2 Pet. 1:3). So if God has designed us with basic needs, then He has provided a way for us to meet those needs and glorify Him at the same time. Our job is to seek Him in the task of meeting our needs, because in doing this, we will glorify Him in the process. "So do not worry, saying, 'What shall we eat?' or 'What shall we drink?' or 'What shall we wear?' For the pagans run after all these things, and your heavenly Father knows that you need them. But seek first His kingdom and His righteousness, and all these things will be given to you, as well. Therefore, do not worry about tomorrow, for tomorrow will worry about itself. Each day has enough trouble of its own" (Matt. 6:31-34).

The concept of motive is natural, normal, and right. As wise and maturing young adults, living away from home and parental supervision, we need to have a plan to check out the source of our motives, and then make a careful plan to meet our needs. Prayerfully read through each area of need. Begin now to develop a plan to check your motives and to meet your true needs. This is not an exhaustive list, but it will help you get started.

I have given you a chart on the next page as an example to follow with some situations to get you started. The list of fundamental needs comes from Abraham Maslow's "Hierarchy of Needs." I have also written a corresponding situation, cost/consequence (By the way, cost is not limited to money it may also include time, energy, relationships, etc.), Biblical factor (What does the Bible have to say about the situation be it command, principle, or blessing?), and alternative (We always have alternatives available to us when making decisions, because by definition decision means choice.)

The example I have given you is only one option and not the only possibility. Work through the remaining items on the chart with a class-mate, your leader, accountability partner, or parent. Then plug in your own situations in the evaluation chart for motives that is on the following page.

Motives Evaluation Chart

Fundamental Need	Given Situations	Cost/Consequence	Biblical Factor	Alternative
Physical need	Ordering Pizza	Do I have the extra money, am I really hungry or just bored, if I buy pizza now will I have the cash I need later	Good Stewardship (Matt. 25:14-30)	Eat in the cafeteria, eat pbj, buy frozen pizza, save the money
Safety need	Carrying mace or other weapons			
Love and Belonging	Join a sorority or fraternity			
Esteem	Maintaining a 4.0 GPA			
Self-Actualization	Double majoring			

Motives Evaluation Chart

Fundamental Need	Given Situations	Cost/Consequence	Biblical Factor	Alternative
Physical need				
Safety need				
Love and Belonging				
Esteem				
Self-Actualization				

Day Four: A "Heart" Exam

Emotions...Why we feel the way we do

Emotions are kind of like motives, hard to define. Even though they are hard to articulate, they are quite real. Emotion is defined as a state of feeling that will have physical, situational, and cognitive elements to it. If we see a sad movie about a dog being run over by a car, our emotional response might be sorrow. The physical response may be tears. The cognitive response might be driving home from the theater at a much slower speed so that we can look out for stray dogs in the street. Frightening situations may provoke a number of emotions; fear, anxiety, sadness, anger etc. Our knowledge about fearful situations might evoke the same types of responses.

College is a very taxing physical, situational, and cognitive transition. The transition to college is compounded when students are not only transitioning to the university campus but to a new country and culture. Many third culture kids (TCKs) either transferred to their host country at an early age or they were born in a country not of their parent's place of origin. So for example, you might have a United States passport, but going stateside might feel more like moving to a foreign country.

Going on stateside assignments (furlough) while growing up may have been returning "home" for your parents, but for you, it might have been more like an extended vacation or a rather long mission trip. Your passport may not be the best indicator of where "home" is for you, and moving to the United States for college may create some never before experienced emotions. You may feel a sense of excitement, as you should, because you are headed to college! You may feel a sense of dread because of all the unknowns. It is possible that you will struggle with feelings of guilt or anger. All of these feelings will come and go; sometimes you will experience them all at once.

There may be times when you feel like your world is turning upside-down and the emotional pressure may make you feel like your head is locked in a vise. It is important to know that this is normal and you can to make it through. God will not give you more than you can handle. He will give you the means to help you through this emotionally difficult time. "No temptation has seized you except what is common to man. And God is faithful; he will not let you

be tempted beyond what you can bear. But when you are tempted, he will also provide a way out so that you can stand up under it."
(1 Cor. 10:13)

In 1969 Dr. Elisabeth Kübler-Ross introduced her five-stage theory concerning grief (primarily in the case of death). She said that grief is the emotional stress caused by any significant transition which is often caused by loss. Moving to college certainly qualifies as a significant transition, especially if you are moving to another country to go to college. There is also a sense of loss that occurs; loss of friendships as you know them, loss of daily family contact, loss of identity, loss of favorite foods, places, and celebrations, the list goes on. Kübler-Ross said that there are five stages of grief. Now just because she uses the word stage that does not mean that these stages happen in any particular order and there is no guarantee how much time each stage will take. All this to say give yourself (and others) a little space and a little grace when you start to experience these things.

Stages of Grief

Denial: This is most commonly the first stage to be experienced. We never want to hear bad news, so when it happens many times our first reaction is not to believe it. When I learned of God's new direction for me and the ministry I was involved in, I didn't want to believe it. After nearly fifteen years in Costa Rica God was leading me to Mexico (not that this was "bad" news). I didn't have anything against Mexico, but Costa Rica was "home." When have you experienced this stage of grief? What were the circumstances involved?

_____
_____
_____
_____
_____
_____
_____
_____

Being Ready

Anger: In this stage, people turn their feelings of anger outward toward persons other than themselves. They, many times, even become angry at God for allowing the loss to happen to them. When I moved from Costa Rica to Mexico, there were times that I felt anger at everyone and everything; not because I hated living in Mexico but because I missed Costa Rica so much. When have you experienced this kind of anger and why do you think it was happening?

_____
_____
_____
_____
_____
_____
_____

Guilt: This stage can incorporate true guilt and/or false guilt. Guilt, in this stage, is anger turned inward (unlike the above stage where it is turned outward). Guilt is often a result of the previous stage, anger. People feel guilty for being angry at others or guilt, because they feel sad. Sometimes people go through a time of saying; "if only I could have…" or "I should have…" I remember the guilt I felt over drinking my last cup of Volio coffee (Costa Rica's best, in my humble opinion). I felt guilty because I cried. Now, my sorrow wasn't because of the coffee (although that might be reason enough – Volio is great coffee). My tears came when I was reminded that I could no longer run down to the market and pick up my favorite coffee… because I was no longer in the place that I had grown to love and considered "home." Have you ever felt guilty about some of your feelings? When? What were the circumstances?

_____
_____
_____
_____
_____
_____
_____

Depression: This stage is also known as the "genuine grief" stage. This is a very important stage. Significant loss and transition is hard on our hearts. God designed tears to be a release valve. It is perfectly healthy to cry. As a matter of fact, a good cry will help keep serious depression at bay. The screen saver on my computer is set to do a slide show of my pictures. The first time that screen saver kicked on, after moving to Mexico, and I saw pictures of Texas, Oklahoma, and Costa Rica I cried like a baby. I was truly bummed for a little while. When was the last time that you wept over a loss? What were the circumstances involved?

_____
_____
_____
_____

Resolution: This is the last stage of grief. It usually comes quickly after the other four stages are worked through. In this stage the desire and excitement for life returns to a person who has experienced loss and major transition. Resolution for me came quickly after moving to Mexico. The students and teachers at my new school were wonderful people and I soon became quite excited about life and ministry in Mexico.

What loss has God taken you through that now you can look back and rejoice over the journey? Explain.

_____
_____
_____
_____
_____

Once again, the stages of grief are not set in concrete. They may occur in a different order. The important thing is not to become overwhelmed when the grief process begins. Be open and honest with what is going on in your life. God loves you and cares for you. You are not alone in this.

Day Five: A Willing Heart

We have looked at what the Bible has to say about human hearts. We have seen how important it is to examine the sin, motives, and emotions of our hearts. To finish out the week, we are going to look at a few practical suggestions to help you to be emotionally prepared for college. I am hoping that these ideas will serve you well and spark your own creative thoughts as you make your hearts willing to embrace this exciting transition.

1. **Closure:**   We talked a little about this in unit two. It is important to say good bye to the people that have been an important part of your life and to tell them how much they mean to you, and why. Don't forget to say good bye to those that were also a part of your regular routine; the lady at the market, the gardener, the man who came to collect newspapers and plastic bottles, and the lady who frequently came by asking for food and used clothes.

It is also a good idea to say good bye to the places and things that are important to you. I know that it might sound a little cheesy to say good bye to places, but trust me, it is invaluable to go back to special places one last time especially if you don't plan on returning to your host country or home town for a while. Go with friends and family to these places and take pictures. If there are several places that you want to go back to; a beach, a camp, a mountain, a volcano, a river, a restaurant, a sports field, a vacation spot, or a special event be sure to plan ahead of time. Begin early to make it special and not rushed. List places that are meaningful to you, the places that you would like to visit again before heading off to college.

_____   _____
_____   _____
_____   _____
_____   _____
_____   _____
_____   _____
_____   _____
_____   _____

A College Preparatory Resource for Third Culture Students

2. **Contact:** Again, we looked at this in unit two. However, it bears repeating. Friendships are precious gifts from God. These special relationships give our lives zest, laughter, tears, joy, adventure, memories, and confidence. Stay in contact with family, friends, teachers, ministers, and even school principals. List e-mail or snail mail addresses of those with whom you want to stay in contact.

_____   _____
_____   _____
_____   _____
_____   _____
_____   _____
_____   _____

3. **Share:** Sharing your experience may sound like a simple concept but often times can be difficult. Emotional adaptation will begin to happen when you can share what you are feeling and experiencing. Find someone with whom you can talk. Be willing to be vulnerable with what you are feeling (even if the tears come). Don't just emotionally fall out with everyone you meet in the student center. Develop relationships where you can be honest and open. Keep in mind that this is not all about you. Don't look for people who will only listen to you and your stories but purpose to be a good listener, as well. Your goal here is to develop relationships. Remember others have their stories to tell. Begin developing good interpersonal skills now so that you can develop good friendships during your college years.

4. **Journal:** Another great way to process what you are thinking and feeling during this transitional time, is to journal. It does not have to become complicated or a part of your homework schedule. You can head your entries by date, event, what God is teaching you, people that you meet, classes that you have, feelings that you are experiencing, or in the form of prayer. Be creative! This is your journal, not a homework assignment. You don't even have to write in one particular language or spell correctly. Journaling also helps you look back and see where God has brought you in the journey.

5. **Connect:** Get involved and connect with people. Even though crawling into a shell or becoming a hermit might be your default mode...don't! College is your chance to come out of your shell and connect with some really great people and organizations. Get involved in a church (many of them have great college ministries). Connect with campus activities, dorm Bible studies, intramural sports teams, special interest clubs, and student ministries groups. What interest do you presently have? List things that you like to do or that you might be interested in exploring while at the university.

_____   _____
_____   _____
_____   _____
_____   _____
_____   _____

These are only five suggestions to help you have good closure and positive transition to a new environment. What are some other things that you think would help you and classmates make the emotional adjustment to college life? Your thoughts might just help someone else.

_____
_____
_____
_____
_____
_____
_____
_____
_____
_____
_____

The Week at a Glance

✝

Objectives

To see how the Bible views the human soul

To understand the significance of being spiritually prepared for college

To explore ways to maintain spiritual growth through college

✝

Verse

"He answered: '"Love the Lord your God with all your heart and with all your soul and with all your strength and with all your mind'; and, 'Love your neighbor as yourself.'"
-Luke 10:27

Unit Four:

Loving with the Soul –

Spiritual Preparation

While they may not be church goers, most North American college students are interested in spiritual things, with a rather high percentage considering themselves to be "godly" or highly religious. Without a doubt you will meet many "spiritual" people on your college campus. It is a part of our design to be spiritual. This is what it means to be made in the image of God. Being spiritual is what separates us from my dog Jake (and all of his pawed, clawed, winged, finned, flippered, friends).

Remember that being spiritual is a part of the design and so is worshiping the One True Living God. You may meet lots of people who are highly spiritual but don't have a clue who God is and who they are in relationship to Him.

Being a spiritual person is not just a "part" of who we are; it is the foundation of who we are in relationship to God and to others. This week we will look at being spiritually prepared for college.

Day One: The "Soul" of the Bible

The word "soul" found in the *Shema* translated is *nephesh* meaning; self, life, inner being of man, seat of the appetites, and activity of the will.[7] In Matthew, the translation from the Greek language is *psuchē*, which means breath, by analogy or figuratively a spirit, the rational soul, by implication vital principle, and mental disposition.[8] The King James Dictionary defines "soul" as; the spiritual, rational and immortal substance in man.[9] The soul of man is his eternal essence, the body will give way but the soul will remain forever (Matt. 10:28). The soul of man is to be highly regarded and protected (Prov. 11:30), because there exist eternal consequences for mislaid loyalties (Matt. 16:24-28). According to the last passage, why is it so important to take care of our souls?

_____

_____

_____

_____

The soul of man expresses his deepest longings for God and his utter dependence upon the Creator; a thirst that only a spiritually rich life can enjoy (Ps. 42:1). It is from the depths of the soul, man attributes His highest praises to God, "Praise the Lord, O my soul; all my inmost being, praise his holy name" (Ps. 103:1). The soul of man can be pliable, tender, and moved to emotion (Ps. 42:11). It is in the soul of man that the deepest healing of God occurs (Ps. 23:3), and rest is granted (Jer. 6:16). Why does God care about our souls? Why should we care about our souls?

_____

_____

_____

---

[7] James Strong, *The New Strong's Expanded Exhaustive Concordance of the Bible*, "soul," 189.

[8] Ibid., 275.

[9] Brandon Staggs, *King James Dictionary*, "soul," (Gdansk: Study Light, 2005), [on-line]; accessed 12 September 2005; available at www.studylight.com; Internet.

In regard to His time on planet earth, Jesus' spirituality was a training process from birth; with education at home (Luke 2:51), in the community (Luke 2:52), in the synagogue (Luke 4:16), in the temple (Luke 2:49), through traditions (Matt. 15:1-6), in His intimate time with the Father (Matt. 14:22-23), and time with man (Matt. 26:18-19). For Jesus Christ, all of life was a spiritual matter, making alive the soul and pointing it in the direction of God. Spirituality was the predominate characteristic of the Son of God. He regarded His body as a temple (John 2:19). He asserted that the only valid form of worship would be that done in "spirit and in truth" (John 4:23). Scripture was the holy textbook of His spiritual teaching and His substance in times of trial (Matt. 4:4). If spirituality was important to Jesus, the Son of God, how much more important should it be to us? Is maintaining healthy spiritual growth important to you? Why or why not?

_____
_____
_____
_____

For many people, Sunday school and church was fine "while growing up." Now that they have their high school diploma and are in college, they believe that they have out-grown the church thing. Do you believe that continuing to grow spiritually during college is important? Why or why not?

_____
_____
_____
_____

What may be some of the greatest challenges of staying on a spiritually growing path, while in college?

_____
_____
_____
_____

Being Ready

Knowing what areas of your spiritual walk are difficult may help you to be prepared for such challenges while on your college campus. Where do you presently struggle in spiritual growth?

A College Preparatory Resource for Third Culture Students

Day Two: Priming our Souls

In our small Oklahoma farm town (less than 300 people, yes people... we did not count the cattle) there were three major things that occupied our time as teenagers; basketball, work, and church. I am sure that school and homework were in there somewhere, but these were the three biggies, with basketball being the number one consumer of time, energy, and passion. On the day of our games, the school hallways were donned with blue and white, proudly displaying Carter "Longhorn" pride. Students and teachers alike found it hard to focus on class work. Hours before the game we would chant, yell, cheer, and "bounce off the walls." By the time, we hit the floor we were "primed" and ready to go. Priming began with preparation long before any of our games or tournaments. Being ready to play began in June with summer league teams. The preparation continued through the early fall with shooting practice at 6:30 a.m. every morning and practice every afternoon. To do something well, passion is not enough. It must be accompanied by preparation and practice.

Our faith walk, as Christians, is much like my little basketball analogy. Living as a Christ-follower is not just about the major events themselves. It involves the preparation. If spiritual maturity were just about the moment we accepted Jesus as Savior, a time of rededication, an intense spiritually moving camp, retreat, or worship service, it would be like a bunch of guys deciding one day to buy uniforms and basketball, then the next day be in the NBA final round play offs. The faith walk of a believer is a process. What you and I do now to develop our faith and spiritually prepare ourselves, will serve us later in life.

The spiritual habits you form as a high school student will have an impact on your spiritual life as a college student. If you are not making a concerted effort to grow spiritually right now, it is highly unlikely that you will do so in college. In preparing this material, I interviewed a number of my former students who are now in college. One of the things that they consistently mentioned was how difficult it was to maintain a healthy spiritual walk while in college. In another interview with a regional mission representative, she agreed with the college students that maintaining a growing, spiritual walk in college was difficult, but not impossible. Often times, what happens is a high school student receives a lot of encouragement to grow spiritually. Those of you who are in Christian homes have the support of your parents and/or siblings. You may have family devotional time on a consistent basis and you are may be involved in church and mission activities. In fact, many of you often lead in several areas of ministry, or have your own ministry projects.

You may be attending a Christian school where Bible study and worship services are a part of the regular schedule, or hooked up with a great youth group or accountability group. All of this is absolutely wonderful!!! However, many students hit the college campus and all of a sudden, they find themselves in a spiritual wasteland; all alone to take full responsibility of their own spiritual survival. Where are you in taking responsibility of your own spiritual growth? Take stock of your spiritual walk.

1. If no one reminded me to read my Bible daily, would I read it?   O yes O no
2. If reading my Bible were not homework, would I read it?   O yes O no
3. Do I willing go to church without force or bribe?   O yes O no
4. Do my prayers consist of thanksgiving and praise?   O yes O no
5. Do my prayers consist of confession and intercession?   O yes O no
6. Would I get up for quiet time rather than hit the snooze?   O yes O no
7. Would I memorize Scripture if it were not for a grade?   O yes O no
8. Have I shared Jesus this week, on my own initiative?   O yes O no
9. Do I consistently give of my resources to God's work?   O yes O no
10. Do I consistently control myself without being reminded to?   O yes O no

A College Preparatory Resource for Third Culture Students

Day Three: Growing from Others

One of the greatest gifts God has given us, as believers, is each other. Paul, the Apostle, paints a great analogy for us in his letter to the Corinthians.

"The body is a unit, though it is made up of many parts; and though all its parts are many, they form one body. So it is with Christ. "For we were all baptized by one Spirit into one body - whether Jews or Greeks, slave or free - and we were all given the one Spirit to drink. Now the body is not made up of one part but of many. If the foot should say, "Because I am not a hand, I do not belong to the body," it would not for that reason cease to be part of the body. And if the ear should say, "Because I am not an eye, I do not belong to the body," it would not for that reason cease to be part of the body. If the whole body were an eye, where would the sense of hearing be? If the whole body were an ear, where would the sense of smell be? But in fact, God has arranged the parts in the body, every one of them, just as he wanted them to be. If they were all one part, where would the body be? As it is, there are many parts, but one body"

-1 Corinthians 12:12-20

We were not designed to live the Christian life on our own. We talked a little about this in unit two. For today's lesson, we are going to take advantage of the "body." Today's lesson will involve you learning from other believers. The assignment is easy. You are to find five people and interview them about their spiritual walk. I already have the questions for you. Keep looking until you find five people who are actively growing in their Christian walk. I will give you three specific people to interview and then you may choose the last two. Remember, the objective is to learn from them so do not debate with them, and do not judge them. Remember we can always learn something from others, great or small. Be open to all that God will teach you through others. Question number five is a personal reflection question for you to answer after each interview.

Being Ready

Family Member

Name: _____ Relationship: _____

1. When did you become a Christian? _____

2. What have you found that helped you grow spiritually?

_____
_____
_____
_____

3. How do you study the Bible?

_____
_____
_____
_____

4. What creative ways have you found to pray?

_____
_____
_____

5. What can I learn from this person about spiritual growth?

_____
_____
_____
_____
_____
_____
_____

A College Preparatory Resource for Third Culture Students

Teacher

Name: _____   Relationship: _____

1. When did you become a Christian? _____

2. What have you found that helped you grow spiritually?

_____
_____
_____
_____

3. How do you study the Bible?

_____
_____
_____
_____

4. What creative ways have you found to pray?

_____
_____
_____
_____

5. What can I learn from this person about spiritual growth?

_____
_____
_____
_____
_____
_____
_____
_____

Being Ready

Minister

Name: _____   Relationship: _____

1. When did you become a Christian? _____

2. What have you found that helped you grow spiritually?

_____
_____
_____
_____

3. How do you study the Bible?

_____
_____
_____
_____

4. What creative ways have you found to pray?

_____
_____
_____

5. What can I learn from this person about spiritual growth?

_____
_____
_____
_____
_____
_____
_____

Other

Name: _____ Relationship: _____

1. When did you become a Christian? _____

2. What have you found that helped you grow spiritually?

_____
_____
_____
_____

3. How do you study the Bible?

_____
_____
_____
_____

4. What creative ways have you found to pray?

_____
_____
_____

5. What can I learn from this person about spiritual growth?

_____
_____
_____
_____
_____
_____
_____

Being Ready

Other

Name: _____   Relationship: _____

1. When did you become a Christian? _____

2. What have you found that helped you grow spiritually?

_____
_____
_____
_____

3. How do you study the Bible?

_____
_____
_____
_____

4. What creative ways have you found to pray?

_____
_____
_____
_____

5. What can I learn from this person about spiritual growth?

_____
_____
_____
_____
_____
_____
_____

A College Preparatory Resource for Third Culture Students

Day Four: Hearing from the Word

I do not know about you, but I love modern technology. Every time a new little gadget comes out on the market, it catches my attention, especially if it has anything at all to do with communication. Relationships are very important to me. Family and friends mean a lot to me. Communication with them is ever so important, especially since I have lived on the mission field for several years. Therefore, whether it is a cell phone, internet device, web cam, text messenger, computer item, or hand-held computer that will help me communicate better, faster, and more accurately, I am "all ears."

As much as I love family and friends and want to communicate with them, I want to hear from my Heavenly Father more. The health and well-being of all my other relationships depends upon the relationship that I have with God. If I am not at peace with God, there is no way that I can be at peace with others. This is a principle I have found throughout Scripture and throughout my life. I must love the Lord my God with all my heart, with all my soul, with all my strength, and with all my mind, before I can hope to love others as I love myself (Matt. 22:37-40). He communicates with us more clearly than any form of modern technology can ever hope. God communicates to us through His written Word, the Bible, with His Holy Spirit to help us with the "translation."

In unit one, I mentioned the spiritual discipline of studying the Bible. Today, we are looking at a simple method of hearing God speak through His written Word. Read any passage of Scripture then the questions. In reading any passage of the Bible, we can be sure to find the answer to one of more of the following. "For the word of God is living and active. Sharper than any double-edged sword, it penetrates even to dividing soul and spirit, joints and marrow; it judges the thoughts and attitudes of the heart" (Heb. 4:12). There are enough pages to practice this method for a whole week.

Being Ready

Passage: _____

1. Is there a promise or promises found in this passage?
_____
_____
_____

2. Is there a warning or warnings found in this passage?
_____
_____
_____

3. Is there a sin addressed in this passage or an example not to follow?
_____
_____
_____

4. Is there a command given, an example to follow, or a principle to live by?
_____
_____
_____

5. Does the passage reveal something about God or about us?
_____
_____
_____
_____
_____
_____

Passage: _____

1. Is there a promise or promises found in this passage?

_____
_____
_____
_____

2. Is there a warning or warnings found in this passage?

_____
_____
_____
_____

3. Is there a sin addressed in this passage or an example not to follow?

_____
_____
_____
_____

4. Is there a command given, an example to follow, or a principle to live by?

_____
_____
_____
_____

5. Does the passage reveal something about God or about us?

_____
_____
_____
_____
_____
_____
_____

Being Ready

Passage: _____

1. Is there a promise or promises found in this passage?

_____
_____
_____
_____

2. Is there a warning or warnings found in this passage?

_____
_____
_____
_____

3. Is there a sin addressed in this passage or an example not to follow?

_____
_____
_____
_____

4. Is there a command given, an example to follow, or a principle to live by?

_____
_____
_____
_____

5. Does the passage reveal something about God or about us?

_____
_____
_____
_____
_____
_____

Passage: _____

1. Is there a promise or promises found in this passage?

_____
_____
_____
_____

2. Is there a warning or warnings found in this passage?

_____
_____
_____
_____

3. Is there a sin addressed in this passage or an example not to follow?

_____
_____
_____
_____

4. Is there a command given, an example to follow, or a principle to live by?

_____
_____
_____
_____

5. Does the passage reveal something about God or about us?

_____
_____
_____
_____
_____
_____

Being Ready

Passage: _____

1. Is there a promise or promises found in this passage?

_____
_____
_____
_____

2. Is there a warning or warnings found in this passage?

_____
_____
_____
_____

3. Is there a sin addressed in this passage or an example not to follow?

_____
_____
_____
_____

4. Is there a command given, an example to follow, or a principle to live by?

_____
_____
_____
_____

5. Does the passage reveal something about God or about us?

_____
_____
_____
_____
_____
_____

Passage: _____

1. Is there a promise or promises found in this passage?

_____
_____
_____
_____

2. Is there a warning or warnings found in this passage?

_____
_____
_____
_____

3. Is there a sin addressed in this passage or an example not to follow?

_____
_____
_____
_____

4. Is there a command given, an example to follow, or a principle to live by?

_____
_____
_____
_____

5. Does the passage reveal something about God or about us?

_____
_____
_____
_____
_____
_____
_____

Being Ready

Passage: _____

1. Is there a promise or promises found in this passage?

_____
_____
_____
_____

2. Is there a warning or warnings found in this passage?

_____
_____
_____
_____

3. Is there a sin addressed in this passage or an example not to follow?

_____
_____
_____
_____

4. Is there a command given, an example to follow, or a principle to live by?

_____
_____
_____
_____

5. Does the passage reveal something about God or about us?

_____
_____
_____
_____
_____
_____

A College Preparatory Resource for Third Culture Students

Day Five: Biblical Basis for Life

In the beautiful southern-most tip of the lush, tropical province of Alajuela, Costa Rica, boasts the quaint town of *Grecia* (Greece). The life of this little town and the center of all activity are like unto the heart of most Costa Rican communities, the church. Unlike in other places, the heart of this town is an odd, red, metal church building. It is odd, because very few churches in Costa Rica are red and it is odd because no others are made completely of iron. The story of the town and church is unique. Like most legends, there is an element of truth and a large portion of imagination. The legend behind the metal church took place when the Americas were very young.

A prince from Belgium decided to visit the western hemisphere. Anticipating his arrival to what he could only imagine as a heathen jungle, the noble, in part, as a gift, and in part, as his own luggage, intended to send his chief builder and his finest crew ahead of him with a replica of a French neo-gothic church. The Belgium government sent the supplies ahead of the crew and chief builder. The shipment arrived at the Port of Limon on the Atlantic side of Costa Rica then made the long journey to its final destination west of the capital city of San Jose where, in the town plaza, the crated prefabricated building sat for ten years. After receiving the coordinates to the mysterious jungle location, the crew and master builder traveled to the west to construct the model church.

The prince continued with his plans of travel, anticipating the comfort of worship in a familiar sanctuary. He arrived in Guatemala, and despite his greatest effort, could not find his church. All the while, the folks in the rain forest of Costa Rica eagerly waited their royal visitor. He never arrived. It was not until years later that the mystery of the foreign "gift" was revealed. It was then, that the church of *Grecia* was presented as a gift from Belgium, expressing friendship and community between the two countries.

In life, we may receive gifts by accident, incorrect coordinates, instructions, or maps. We may have the greatest intentions in the world and think that we are communicating our message and directions clearly, only to find out that our "church" was sent to the wrong country. Unlike human communication, divine communication is always clear. We do not have to worry about wrong coordinates when we search deeply and honestly into the Word of God, the teaching of Jesus, and the direction of the Holy Spirit. From the daunting details of the laws of Leviticus, to the precepts of the Psalms, and to the Spirit-led, example-driven divine laws of the New Testament pages, God lead His people with clarity.

The Bible reveals God. His Spirit helps us to understand this revelation. It reveals His hope for humanity, His purposes, His glory, and how we can reflect His glory. God is consistent throughout His interaction in human history. There is no guesswork when it comes to God and His plan for creation. The Bible is our reliable resource for divine direction and guidance. It is our blueprint and our final evaluation for the Christian life.

A contractor of the highest integrity will go to great pains to select the finest of materials for his project. True artisanship does not compromise the quality of the masterpiece for economic savings. A jeweler will invest years searching for the perfect gem to complete his prized display. He may travel continents in pursuit of a flawless stone. He may even sell all to gain the illusive treasure.

The formative years of the human mind are like unto a great project awarded to the master builder. Only the highest quality of materials is acceptable and only the most skilled artisan will adequately suffice for the daunting task of education. Like the treasured jewel, flawlessness and perfection are the minimum requirements for a Christian's education. The only appropriate foundational element for a Christ-centered education is God's Holy Word. "Every word of God is flawless; He is a shield to those who take refuge in Him" (Prov. 30:5). Programs may be flawed, schedules limited, resources inadequate, teachers, students, principals, parents who are fallible, but a Christian's college education built on the teachings, commands, and principles of the infallible Word of God will be a shining jewel in a perfectly constructed hall dedicated to honoring God Most High.

The Week at a Glance

Objectives

To see how the Bible views the human body and strength

To understand the significance of being physically prepared for college

To explore ways to maintain physical health while in college

Verse

"For physical training is of some value, but godliness has value for all things, holding promise for both the present life and the life to come."

- 1 Timothy 4:8

Unit Five: Loving with Strength – Physical Preparation

The final word of the *Shema*, as seen in Deuteronomy, is the word strength (Deut. 6:4-5). The word's intended meaning pertains as much to the physical aspect of life as it pertains to the sheer might, force, abundance, diligence, and exceeding power of the human will.[10] It is the aspiration of man to be like Christ in His humanity. Jesus left the glories of heaven and took the humble form of a human being, with the full understanding of what it means to be human (Phil. 2:5-11).

He grew as man does (Luke 2:52). He was well acquainted with the sickness, suffering, and death that the human body experiences (Matt. 9:1-34). Jesus was also familiar with the sheer strength of the human heart, He exemplified the power of its tenacity through His sufferings (John 19:28-42). Jesus was completely human with a completely human frame subject to all the ills of the human existence, yet without sin (1 John 3:5). This week we will address loving God and others with physical strength and strength of will by: seeing the body as the Bible does, understanding the physical dynamics of being healthy.

---

[10] James Strong, *The New Strong's Expanded Exhaustive Concordance of the Bible,* "strength", 145.

Being Ready

Day One: The "Body" of the Bible

    Paul explains to Christians that there is some benefit in training the body. However, the eternal investment that comes from godliness brought through spiritual training is of much greater value (1Tim. 4:8). Paul reminds the church that the physical body is of significant importance to its Creator.

    The evidence is found in the fact that the physical body of a believer serves as the temple of the Holy Spirit; "Do you not know that your body is a temple of the Holy Spirit, who is in you, whom you have received from God? You are not your own; you were bought at a price. Therefore, honor God with your body" (1 Cor. 6:19-20). Paul warns Christ-followers not to offer the parts of their bodies to sin lest they become slaves to sin. "Do not offer the parts of your body to sin, as instruments of wickedness, but rather offer yourselves to God, as those who have been brought from death to life; and offer the parts of your body to him as instruments of righteousness" (Rom. 6:13).

1. As Christians, who really has the last "say-so" when it comes to our bodies? (Hint: 1 Cor. 6:19) _____

2. What is the purpose of our bodies according to Romans 6:13?
_____

3. Read the rest of this chapter, Romans 6:13-23. Are we living under grace or under the law (Law of Moses) according to this passage? _____

4. For those who are believers, are we slaves to sin or slaves to righteousness?
_____
_____

5. What is the result of continuing to be a slave to sin?
_____
_____

6. What are the results of begin a salve to righteousness?
_____
_____

    The point that Paul is trying to make here is that we are going to be slaves either to sin which results in ultimate eternal death or to righteousness, which leads to ultimate eternal life. You do not have to be a college graduate to figure this one out! Our bodies are temporal things. Although their desires are strong, they are short-lived. This is the question we have to ask ourselves; "Is the eternal payoff worth the short-term choices we make?"

    The moment of temptation is not the time to make these decisions. Deciding whether to buy a term paper, hours before it is due, is not the time. Deciding whether to get plastered with your frat friends on the way to a Greek party is not the time. Deciding whether to have sex with someone you are dating while in the throws of passionate kissing is not the time to decide to be a slave to sin or righteousness. This decision comes **LONG** before any of these situations or others like them arise. The choice to be a slave to righteousness is now! Choosing this option steers you away from lots of last minute decisions. It is the last minute decisions that often get us into trouble. When counseling with those who are dealing with the consequences of bad decisions and the result of sin in their lives, I always hear in one form or another, "I don't know how it happened. I didn't mean for it to happen that way. I didn't start out planning to sin" and the list goes on.

    The decision for righteousness means that you are planning. Because you are becoming an independent young adult, you will not have the benefit of your parents making sure you get your homework done, making sure you are in by curfew, or monitoring your relationships. You have to make choices that will set you up for success in the righteousness department. Decide, before the due date to schedule your time in such a way that you get the term paper finished. You may have to forego hanging out with friends until after the paper is finished, but you will not have to deal with the temptation to cheat later. Decide, before the option of the beer bash, what friends are good and healthy for you; those who will walk with you in the path of righteousness. Decide before the passionate kissing, what the healthy physical and emotional boundaries are to be in a relationship.

Being Ready

While the Bible speaks of the physical strength of man, and the devotion to be rendered to God with that strength (Deut. 6:5), Scripture also addresses the dependence of man upon the strength of the Lord (Ps. 46:1). Strength is found in worship, praise, and song lifted to God (Exod. 15:2). "The joy of the Lord is your strength" (Neh. 8:10). A true sense of strength and refuge is encountered in God for the weary soul (Ps. 46:1). The strength of man is renewed and fortified in waiting upon the Lord (Isa. 40:31). A number of passages in the Psalms speak to the might and strength of God (Ps. 24:8, 50:1, 89:8, 136:12, 147:5). It is clear that while God granted man some physical and mental fortitude, true strength comes to man through the resources of his Creator.

1. How are you depending on God as your strength?

_____
_____
_____

2. In what areas of your life do you need to depend more on God's strength?

_____
_____
_____
_____
_____
_____
_____

3. Now is the time to decide to live for righteousness or sinfulness. What say you? Every time we are faced with the truth of Scripture, we make a decision to respond in obedience or to respond in disobedience. Remember that delayed obedience is disobedience. In light of our study today, will you trust in the strength of God to help you live a righteous life, or will you choose to follow your own plan? Use the following lines to write a prayer to God concerning what you have decided, to be a slave to righteousness or a slave to sinfulness.

Dear God-

Day Two: Body
Eating Well

If I could boil physical fitness down to three basic concepts it would be eating well, exercising well, and sleeping well. Let us start with eating well. Nearly every website pertaining to college and eating, mentions the infamous "freshman fifteen." This is the legendary fifteen pounds that freshman (mainly females...sorry girls) gain during their first year of college. However, in preparing for this study, the most dependable reports say the average college freshman gains around five pounds.

Whew, that is a little better than fifteen! By-and-**LARGE,** you are not doomed to the curse of any extra poundage just because you are pursuing a high education. The added weight gain is often attributed to more time in the books and less time on the field or on the court. Another major contributor to "mass" is the amount of fast food and junk food that college students take in. When you were at home, most of you had the blessing of home-cooking! Oh, those were the days... when someone who loved you, prepared well balanced and nutritious meals (most of which didn't come out of a box, a can, the freezer, or the drive thru). Parents are also great about helping you monitor calorie intake. I know it might have driven you crazy when you where in high school, having your parents push the second helping away or the dessert even further away, but they were looking out for you because they love you. Soon you will have all kinds of freedom (food is just one area). With this freedom comes responsibility.

Our bodies are beautiful works of art. God sculptured us just right. Now, with His help, we are to maintain these masterpieces, especially if you are a Christian. Do you remember this passage from yesterday? "Do you not know that your body is a temple of the Holy Spirit, who is in you, whom you have received from God? You are not your own; you were bought at a price. Therefore, honor God with your body" (1 Cor. 6:19-20). Since we are managers of God's property, we need to be responsible. We will start by taking inventory. For the rest of the week, record what you are eating. Evaluate your choices with the following ten items. Award yourself with a point for each category for each day.

Ask yourself these questions:

1. Did I eat only until satisfied or did I overeat?

2. Did I make the healthiest choice when I had the opportunity to?

3. Did I eat several small meals through out the day instead of one or two huge meals?

4. Did I eat from all of the food groups (USDA food groups that is, contrary to popular belief…chocolate is not a food group)? Reference the US government's "my pyramid" website for this portion of the assignment.

5. Did my meals include proteins, carbohydrates, and fruits and veggies?

6. Did I take in the right number of calories for my age and activity level? Use calorie calculators of which can be found on any number of websites to help determine how many calories you need daily.

7. Did I eat alone, while studying, or while "on the run"?

8. Did I drink enough water? Your actual need will vary; again you can determine your water intake need by using a reliable internet source.

9. Did I eat a variety of foods each meal?

10. Did I thank God for the gift of food and drink?

	Tuesday	**10 points covered**
Breakfast		
Snack		
Lunch		
Snack		
Supper		
Snack		

A College Preparatory Resource for Third Culture Students

	Wednesday	**10 points covered**
Breakfast		
Snack		
Lunch		
Snack		
Supper		
Snack		

	Thursday	10 points covered
Breakfast		
Snack		
Lunch		
Snack		
Supper		
Snack		

	Friday	10 points covered
Breakfast		
Snack		
Lunch		
Snack		
Supper		
Snack		

Day Three: Body

Exercising Well

Playing is not just for kids. Our bodies are designed to move, and move they must! Exercise is not a dirty word (unless you are thinking in terms of sweat). Another contributing factor to unhealthy weight gain is the change to a sedentary lifestyle. As you become more involved in your major and minor areas of study, you will find yourself reading, studying, and writing more…all, while sitting. Another thing to consider is that many more students are involved in organized sports during high school than during college. You don't have to be on a collegiate athletic team to stay in shape. Take the soccer ball with you to college. Most schools have intramural sports teams. Even if your university does not have sports clubs or organized intramural teams take your ball or your Frisbee in the park and start playing. This is a great way to meet people. It would be a good idea if you invite someone (like your roommate) out to kick the ball around or toss the Frisbee. If you are tossing a Frisbee around and chasing it down by yourself you might look a little like my dog when he is bored and plays by himself.

College is a great time to discover lots of things about the world that God created and about the "you" He created. Before going to college, I played basketball, volleyball, and softball. All of these were organized high school sports. Really these were about the only sports that I thought existed (Remember that I hail from a small town). When I got to college, I discovered tennis, swimming, running, and rock climbing. Discover the athlete in you.

I understand that not everyone may be as excited about exercise as I am. Many of you may be physically challenged when it comes to sports and exercise in general. Some of you may just hate it and cringe at the thought of having to move your bodies any faster than is absolutely necessary. I understand. Let me offer a couple of ideas that might make it easier.

Thinking of Exercise

1. Think of exercise as a form of worship, honoring God by maintaining the temple He has given you.
2. Find a friend to keep you accountable to exercise (Someone who is a little more motivated than you).
3. Schedule workouts like you would your quiet time (Keep both commitments faithfully).
4. Plan to exercise early in the day (You get it out of the way and then you are free to do other things. It also helps get your blood pumping and brain cells working…and you are going to need that in college).
5. Use exercise as study breaks, walk around campus in between studying for tests and reading all those assignments.
6. Download music or audio books on your MP3 and hop on the treadmill. Before you know it, you have walked an hour, while singing to your favorite tunes, taken a study break, and finished (reading) "The Divine Comedy."
7. Walk more places. If it is safe walk to class, to the store, to the library, up the stairs, to church, to friend's dorms, to the mall, etc.
8. Reward yourself for exercising (not necessarily with food, you don't want to walk three miles, burn three hundred calories, and then eat a thousand calories of ice cream). Rewards like a movie, extra hours of sleep, that new "something" you have been wanting, or the knowledge that you are healthier, honoring God, and are going to look and feel great.
9. Be consistent.
10. Remember 1 Corinthians 6:19-20.

Being Ready

1. What is your personal philosophy of exercise and fitness?

_____
_____
_____
_____
_____
_____
_____

2. What sports or forms of exercise do you presently practice on a regular basis?

_____
_____
_____
_____

3. What sports or activities have you always wanted to try or play?

_____
_____
_____
_____

4. Which of the ten ideas on the previous pages would you be willing to begin?

_____
_____
_____
_____
_____
_____
_____

5. Rewrite 1 Corinthians 6:19-20 in your own words.

Day Four: Body

Sleeping Well

Of the three; eating right, exercising consistently, and getting enough Zzz the latter might be the hardest to do. It almost always seems like there is more to do in the day than day to do it all in. Between studying for Western Philosophy class, writing British Literature book reviews, and snoring roommates, the night hours seem to just slip by. Then one day you find yourself drooling on the desk or your notebook between the bibliographies and the reference section of the library, waking to find spiral notebook impressions on your face. Oh sweet slumber!

College is an exciting time. There are lots of exciting experiences to have, lots of big responsibilities, lots of new found independence and freedom, lots of great people to meet, and LOTS of hard studying to do. You may find yourself pulling "all-nighters" and consuming large amounts of caffeine to try to get it all in. However, our bodies were not made for this type of abuse, especially if it is prolonged. Our bodies and brains need a night of sleep to recover from the demands of the day. Do not underestimate the importance of sleep! It is nearly impossible to maintain emotional, spiritual, physical, and cognitive health on three to four hours of sleep a night. You really need to average more hours of sleep a night.

Research has shown that continual lack of adequate sleep will result in many counterproductive elements for a young scholar. "Inadequate sleep can cause decreases in: performance, concentration, reaction times, consolidation of information learning and can cause increases in: memory lapses, accidents and injuries, behavior problems, and mood problems."[11] Now, it stands to reason that if you invested four years of high school preparing for college that time, money, energy (emotional and intellectual), and much prayer enrolling in a college degree program, that you not blow it by sleeping through class. All the items listed in the statement from the National Heart, Lung, and Blood Institute (performance, concentration, reaction times, memory, and consolidation of information learning…not to mention your physical safety and emotional stability) are all absolute necessities in college.

---

[11] National Heart, Lung, and Blood Institute, "For Parents: Why Sleep is So Important," *Star Sleeper,* (Bethesda: National Heart, Lung, and Blood Institute, 2006) [on-line]; accessed 18 February 2006; available from http://www.nhlbi.nih.gov/health/public/sleep/starslp/parents/whysleep.htm; Internet.

It would be a shame to stay up for thirty-six hours studying for a Biology test only to arrive at the wrong class, start taking a Psychology test (a class of which you are not even enrolled) with the only writing utensil you can find a pink highlighter in your pajama's pocket…because you left in such a hurry you forgot to change clothes, realize your mistake, run out of the class down the hall, crash into the door (minor concussion), finally get the right test in hand…then draw an utter blank on the first line…Name and Date.

Bottom line…Get enough Sleep!

Day Five: The Body and Stress

With the changes in our lives there is always the element of stress, and stress can affect our health. Stress is not necessarily a bad thing, but like everything, it has its place and that is under the Lordship of Jesus Christ. When stress is mounting, one of the most important things we can keep in mind is who we are in Christ. Just before his crucifixion Jesus gathered with his disciples. Because Jesus knew where He came from, who He belonged to, who He was, and where He was going, he could wash the feet of the disciples and later wash their sins and our sins away with his blood.

"It was just before the Passover Feast. Jesus knew that the time had come for Him to leave this world and go to the Father. Having loved His own who were in the world, He now showed them the full extent of His love. The evening meal was being served, and the devil had already prompted Judas Iscariot, son of Simon, to betray Jesus. Jesus knew that the Father had put all things under His power, and that He had come from God and was returning to God; so He got up from the meal, took off His outer clothing, and wrapped a towel around His waist. After that, He poured water into a basin and began to wash His disciples' feet, drying them with the towel that was wrapped around Him"

-John 13:1-5

You are a child of God and that means so much. When the pressure is building up in our lives, it is so easy to focus on the moment and to develop a distorted viewpoint of the present situation. Knowing who we are often puts things back into perspective for us. These moments are fading. Life on this planet is temporal, and we need to keep in mind that we are eternal beings. Review what the Bible has to say about who you are as a child of God. Read each of the statements on the following pages aloud. Remember that there will always be stress, and reciting these passages is not a magical formula to rid you of stress they are only reminders of who you are in Christ.

Who I am in Jesus...

This child of God	Is able - Philippians 4:13
This child of God	Is abounding in grace - 2 Corinthians 9:8
This child of God	Is abounding in hope - Romans 15:4, 13
This child of God	Is Abraham's offspring - Galatians 3:29
This child of God	Is abundant - John 10:10
This child of God	Is accepted - Ephesians 1:6
This child of God	has access - Ephesians 2:18
This child of God	Is adequate - 2 Corinthians 3:5
This child of God	Is adopted - Ephesians 1:5
This child of God	Is alive - Ephesians 2:4-5
This child of God	Is an ambassador for Christ - 2 Corinthians 5:20
This child of God	Is anointed - 1 John 2:20
This child of God	Is anxious for nothing - Philippians 4:6
This child of God	Is the apple of His eye - Zechariah 2:8
This child of God	Is appointed by God - John 15:16
This child of God	Is the aroma of Christ - 2 Corinthians 2:15
This child of God	Is not ashamed - 2 Timothy 1:12
This child of God	Is assured of reward - 1 Corinthians 15:58
This child of God	Is assured of success - Proverbs 16:3
This child of God	has authority over the devil - Luke 9:1
This child of God	Is baptized into Christ - 1 Corinthians 12:15
This child of God	Is beautiful - Psalm 149:4
This child of God	Is becoming a mature person - Ephesians 4:13
This child of God	Is becoming conformed to Christ - Romans 8:29
This child of God	Is a believer - Romans 10:9
This child of God	belongs to God - John 17:9
This child of God	Is betrothed - Hosea 2:19-20
This child of God	Is blameless - 1 Corinthians 1:8
This child of God	Is blessed - Ephesians 1:3
This child of God	Is blood bought - 1 Corinthians 6:19-20
This child of God	Is bold - Proverbs 28:1
This child of God	Is a bondservant - Psalm 116:16
This child of God	Is born of God - 1 John 5:18
This child of God	Is born again - 1 Peter 1:23
This child of God	Is bought with a price - 1 Corinthians 6:20
This child of God	Is a branch of the True Vine - John 15:5
This child of God	Is His bride - Isaiah 54:5
This child of God	Is His brother - Hebrews 2:11

Being Ready

This child of God	Is brought near - Ephesians 2:13
This child of God	Is built up - 1 Peter 2:5
This child of God	Is buried with Christ - Romans 6:4
This child of God	Is called - 1 Peter 5:10
This child of God	Is calm - Philippians 4:6
This child of God	Is cared for - 1 Peter 5:7
This child of God	Is carried - Exodus 19:4
This child of God	Is changed - 1 Samuel 10:6
This child of God	Is a child of God - John 1:12
This child of God	Is cherished - Ephesians 5:29
This child of God	Is chosen - 1 Peter 2:9
This child of God	Is circumcised spiritually - Colossians 2:11
This child of God	Is a citizen of heaven - Philippians 3:20
This child of God	Is clay in the potter's hand - Jeremiah 18:6
This child of God	Is clean - Ezekiel 36:25; John 15:3
This child of God	Is cleansed - 1 John 1:7,9
This child of God	Is clothed with Christ - Galatians 3:27
This child of God	Is a co-heir with Christ - Romans 8:17
This child of God	Is comforted - Jeremiah 31:13
This child of God	Is complete in Christ - Colossians 2:10
This child of God	Is confident - 1 John 4:17
This child of God	Is confident of answers to prayer - 1 John 5:14-15
This child of God	Is confident He will finish me - Philippians 1:6
This child of God	Is confident He will never leave me - Hebrews 13:5-6
This child of God	Is a conqueror - Romans 8:37
This child of God	Is content - Philippians 4:11
This child of God	Is content with weakness - 2 Corinthians 12:10
This child of God	Is continually with God - Psalm 73:23
This child of God	Is controlled by the love of Christ - 2 Corinthians 12:10
This child of God	Is courageous - 1 Chronicles 28:20
This child of God	Is created in Christ for good works - Ephesians 2:10
This child of God	Is created in His image - Genesis 1:27
This child of God	Is crucified with Him - Galatians 2:20
This child of God	Is dead in Christ - Romans 6:4
This child of God	Is dead to sin - Romans 6:11
This child of God	Is a delight - Psalm 147:11
This child of God	Is delighted in - Isaiah 42:1
This child of God	Is delivered - Psalm 107:6
This child of God	Is desired - Psalm 45:11
This child of God	Is determined - Philippians 4:13
This child of God	Is a disciple - John 8:31-32

This child of God	Is disciplined - Hebrews 12:5-11
This child of God	Is drawing near with confidence - Hebrews 4:16
This child of God	Is empowered to obey - Philippians 2:13
This child of God	Is encouraged - 2 Thessalonians 2:16-17
This child of God	Is enlightened - Ephesians 1:18
This child of God	Is enriched in everything - 1 Corinthians 1:5
This child of God	Is equipped - 2 Timothy 3:16-17
This child of God	Is established Deuteronomy 28:9
This child of God	has eternal life - John 3:36
This child of God	has every good thing - Philemon 6
This child of God	Is exalted at His right hand - Acts 2:34-35
This child of God	Is faithful - Revelation 17:14
This child of God	Is family - Psalm 68:5
This child of God	Is far from oppression - Isaiah 54:14
This child of God	Is favored - Job 10:12
This child of God	Is a fellow citizen with the saints - Ephesians 2:19
This child of God	Is a fellow worker - Colossians 4:11
This child of God	Is filled - Acts 2:4
This child of God	Is filled to the fullness of God - Colossians 2:9-10
This child of God	Is filled with the fruit of righteousness - Philippians 1:11
This child of God	Is filled with the fruit of the Spirit - Galatians 5:22-23
This child of God	Is filled with the knowledge of His will - Colossians 1:9
This child of God	Is filled with joy - John 17:13
This child of God	Is a finished product -in progress - Philippians 1:6
This child of God	Is a first fruit - Romans 8:23
This child of God	Is forgiven - Ephesians 1:7
This child of God	Is formed in the womb by God - Jeremiah 1:5
This child of God	was lost, but now is found - Luke 19:10
This child of God	Is a fragrance - 1 Corinthians 1:15-16
This child of God	Is free - John 8:36
This child of God	Is freely given all things - Romans 8:32
This child of God	Is gifted - Romans 12:6
This child of God	Is given His magnificent promises - 2 Peter 1:3-4
This child of God	Is given His Holy Spirit - 2 Corinthians 1:22
This child of God	Is glorified with Him - 2 Thessalonians 2:14
This child of God	Is God's child - John 1:12
This child of God	Is God's gift to Christ - John 17:24
This child of God	knows God is for me - Romans 8:31
This child of God	Is gracious - Proverbs 22:11
This child of God	Is granted grace in Christ Jesus - Romans 5:17,20
This child of God	Is guarded by God - 2 Timothy 1:12

Being Ready

This child of God	Is guarded by God's peace - Philippians 4:7
This child of God	Is guaranteed - Ephesians 1:13-14
This child of God	Is guided - Psalm 48:14
This child of God	Is guiltless - Romans 8:1
This child of God	Is the head - Deuteronomy 28:13
This child of God	Is healed - 1 Peter 2:24
This child of God	Is healthy - Deuteronomy 7:15
This child of God	Is an heir of God - Titus 3:7
This child of God	Is helped by Him - Isaiah 44:2
This child of God	Is hidden with Christ in God - Colossians 3:3
This child of God	Is His - Isaiah 43:1
This child of God	Is His handiwork - Ephesians 2:10
This child of God	Is holy - Ephesians 1:4
This child of God	Is honored - 2 Timothy 2:21
This child of God	Is humble -Philippians 2:24
This child of God	Is the image of God - Genesis 1:27
This child of God	Is the image and glory of God - 1 Corinthians 11:7
This child of God	Is an imitator of God - Ephesians 5:1
This child of God	Is in Christ Jesus - 1 Corinthians 1:30
This child of God	Is included - Ephesians 1:13
This child of God	Is indestructible - John 6:51
This child of God	Is indwelt by Christ Jesus - John 14:20
This child of God	Is indwelt by His Spirit - Romans 8:11
This child of God	Is inscribed on His palms - Isaiah 49:16
This child of God	Is inseparable from His love - Romans 8:35
This child of God	Is an instrument of righteousness - Romans 6:13
This child of God	Is joyful - Philippians 4:4
This child of God	Is justified - Acts 13:39
This child of God	Is kept - Isaiah 38:17
This child of God	Is in a Kingdom of priests - Revelation 1:6
This child of God	Is a king's kid - Psalm 44:4
This child of God	knows all things work together for good - Romans 8:28
This child of God	knows in Whom he believes - 2 Timothy 1:12
This child of God	Is known - 2 Timothy 2:19
This child of God	lacks no wisdom - James 1:5
This child of God	Is lavished with riches of His grace - Ephesians 1:7-8
This child of God	Is led in Christ's triumph - 2 Corinthians 2:14
This child of God	Is liberated - Romans 6:23
This child of God	has life abundant - 1 John 4:9; John 10:10
This child of God	has life and peace in the Spirit - Romans 8:6
This child of God	has light - John 8:12

This child of God	Is a light in a dark place - Acts 13:47
This child of God	has life flowing through me - John 7:38
This child of God	Is like a watered garden - Isaiah 58:11
This child of God	Is a living stone in a spiritual house - 1 Peter 2:5
This child of God	Is the Lord's - Isaiah 44:5
This child of God	Is loved - John 3:16
This child of God	Is loved constantly, unconditionally - Isaiah 43:4
This child of God	Is loyal - Psalm 86:2
This child of God	Is made by Him - Psalm 100:3
This child of God	Is a magnifier of God - Psalm 69:30
This child of God	Is marked - Ephesians 1:13
This child of God	Is a member of His body - Ephesians 5:30
This child of God	Is might in God - Luke 10:19
This child of God	has the mind of Christ - 1 Corinthians 2:16
This child of God	Is a minister - 2 Corinthians 3:6
This child of God	Is a minister of reconciliation - 2 Corinthians 5:18-19
This child of God	Is a mountain mover - Mark 11:22-23
This child of God	Is named - Isaiah 43:1
This child of God	Is near to God - Ephesians 2:13
This child of God	Is never forsaken - Hebrews 13:5
This child of God	Is new - Ephesians 4:24
This child of God	Is new born - 1 Peter 2:2
This child of God	Is a new creation - 2 Corinthians 5:17
This child of God	has new life - Romans 6:4
This child of God	Is part of a new race - 1 Peter 2:9
This child of God	Is not condemned - Romans 8:1
This child of God	Is no longer a slave to sin - Romans 6:6
This child of God	has not been given a spirit of fear - 1 Timothy 1:7
This child of God	Is obedient - Isaiah 1:19
This child of God	Is an object of mercy - Romans 9:23
This child of God	has obtained an inheritance - Ephesians 1:11
This child of God	Is of God's household - Ephesians 2:19
This child of God	Is on the winning side - Colossians 2:15
This child of God	Is one with Him - John 17:23-24
This child of God	Is an overcomer - 1 John 5:4-5
This child of God	Is pardoned - Jeremiah 33:8
This child of God	Is a partaker of Christ - Hebrews 3:14
This child of God	Is a partaker of the Holy Spirit - Hebrews 6:4
This child of God	Is a partaker of grace - Philippians 1:7
This child of God	Is a partaker of the promise in Christ - Ephesians 3:6
This child of God	has passed from death to life - John 5:24

Being Ready

This child of God	Is patient - James 5:8
This child of God	has peace - Philippians 4:7
This child of God	Is one of the people of God - 1 Peter 2:9
This child of God	Is being perfected - 1 Peter 5:10
This child of God	Is pleasing to God - Psalm 149:4
This child of God	Is God's own possession - Titus 2:14
This child of God	Is possessor of all things - 1 Corinthians 3:21-23
This child of God	has the power of God behind me - Philippians 3:21
This child of God	has power - Acts 1:8
This child of God	has power over the devil - Luke 9:1
This child of God	Is predestined - Ephesians 1:11
This child of God	Is prepared beforehand for glory - Romans 9:23
This child of God	Is prosperous - Psalm 1:3
This child of God	Is protected - Psalm 91:14
This child of God	Is provided for - Matthew 6:33
This child of God	Is purchased - Revelation 5:9
This child of God	Is purposeful - Psalm 138:8
This child of God	Is qualified - Colossians 1:12
This child of God	Is raised up with Christ - Ephesians 2:6
This child of God	Is ransomed with Him - Isaiah 35:10
This child of God	Is rare - Proverbs 20:15
This child of God	has received mercy - 1 Peter 2:10
This child of God	has received an unshakable Kingdom - Hebrews 12:28
This child of God	Is reconciled to God - Romans 5:10
This child of God	Is redeemed - Galatians 3:13
This child of God	Is refined - Isaiah 48:10
This child of God	Is reigning with Him - Romans 5:17
This child of God	Is rejoicing - Romans 5:2-3
This child of God	Is renewed - 2 Corinthians 4:16
This child of God	Is His representative - Matthew 5:16
This child of God	Is rescued - Colossians 1:13
This child of God	has rest provided - Matthew 11:28-30
This child of God	Is rewarded by God - Isaiah 49:4
This child of God	Is rich - 2 Corinthians 8:9
This child of God	Is righteous - Ephesians 4:22
This child of God	Is rooted and built up in Him - Colossians 2:7
This child of God	Is royalty - Romans 5:17; 8:16-17
This child of God	Is a royal priesthood - 1 Peter 2:9
This child of God	Is safe - Psalm 4:8
This child of God	Is a saint of God - Psalm 34:9
This child of God	Is the salt of the earth - Matthew 5:13

This child of God	Is sanctified - 1 Corinthians 6:11
This child of God	Is satisfied - Jeremiah 31:14
This child of God	Is saved - Ephesians 2:8
This child of God	Is sealed by God with His Holy Spirit - Ephesians 1:13
This child of God	Is seated with Him - Ephesians 2:6
This child of God	Is secure - Deuteronomy 33:12
This child of God	Is sent - John 20:21
This child of God	Is set free - John 8:31-32,36
This child of God	Is sharing Christ's inheritance - Romans 8:17
This child of God	Is sharing His glory - John 17:22,24
This child of God	Is His sheep - Psalm 23:1
This child of God	Is sheltered - Psalm 91:1
This child of God	Is shielded - Psalm 91:4
This child of God	Is a slave to righteousness - Romans 6:18
This child of God	Is His soldier - 2 Timothy 2:3-4
This child of God	Is a son of God - Romans 8:14
This child of God	Is stable - Isaiah 33:6
This child of God	Is standing in His grace - Romans 5:2
This child of God	Is standing firm in Christ - 2 Corinthians 1:21
This child of God	has my steps established by the Lord - Psalm 37:23
This child of God	Is strengthened in Him - Ephesians 3:16
This child of God	Is strong in the Lord - 1 Corinthians 1:8
This child of God	Is amply supplied - Philippians 4:18
This child of God	Is sustained from birth - Psalm 71:6
This child of God	Is a temple - 1 Corinthians 3:16
This child of God	Is thought about - Psalm 139:17-18
This child of God	Is transferred into His Kingdom - Colossians 1:13
This child of God	Is transformed - 2 Corinthians 3:18
This child of God	Is treasured - Psalm 83:3
This child of God	Is triumphant - 2 Corinthians 2:14
This child of God	Is unafraid - Isaiah 44:2; 51:12
This child of God	Is understood - Ephesians 1:8
This child of God	Is united with Christ - Romans 6:5
This child of God	Is upheld - Psalm 37:17
This child of God	Is upright - Psalm 7:10
This child of God	Is unblemished - Colossians 1:22
This child of God	has understanding - 2 Timothy 2:7
This child of God	Is useful for His glory - Isaiah 43:7
This child of God	Is valuable - Luke 12:24
This child of God	lives in victory - 1 Corinthians 15:57
This child of God	Is walking in His light - 1 John 1:7

Being Ready

This child of God	Is a warrior - 2 Corinthians 10:4
This child of God	Is washed - Titus 3:5
This child of God	Is watching for His return - Luke 12:37
This child of God	Is weak, then is strong - 2 Corinthians 12:10
This child of God	Is in a wealthy place - Psalm 66:12
This child of God	Is welcome - Luke 11:9
This child of God	Is being made whole - Mark 5:34
This child of God	puts on the whole armor of God - Ephesians 6:11
This child of God	Is wise - Proverbs 2:6
This child of God	Is His witness - Acts 1:8
This child of God	Is His workmanship - Ephesians 2:10
This child of God	Is not of this world - John 17:14
This child of God	Is His worshipper - Psalm 95:6
This child of God	Is worthy - Revelation 3:4
This child of God	Is yielded to God - Romans 6:13
This child of God	Is yoked with Jesus - Matthew 11:29
This child of God	Is heaven bound, guaranteed. - I Peter 1: 4

The Week at a Glance

†

Objectives

To see how the Bible views the human mind

To understand the significance of being intellectually prepared for college

To explore ways to make the most out the mind during college

†

Verse

"You will keep in perfect peace him whose mind is steadfast, because he trusts in you. Trust in the LORD forever, for the LORD, the LORD, is the Rock eternal."
        -Isaiah 26:3-4

Unit Six:

Loving with the Mind –

Intellectual Preparation

During the average four years one is in college significant intellectual changes occur, most of which are considered to be developmental in nature but are greatly enhanced by cognitive stimulation and an intercultural environment. Because the intellectual growth is so significant during the college years, universities need to be authorities of their own subject matter, philosophies, missions, and direction because the purpose of higher education is for the benefit of a students' learning. As well, students need to take full advantage of these experts.

With so much to learn, where is the beginning point. Education, in the true sense of the definition, must be subject to Biblical scrutiny and the authority of God. Whether it is Biology or Bible, there exists no knowledge apart from Jesus Christ. He is the author and completer of all true knowledge. All understanding and wisdom begins and ends with Him. This week we will look at loving God and man with the mind, and intellectual preparation.

Day One: The "Mind" of the Bible

Strong's concordance defines the use of the word "mind" in Matthew as being *dianoia,* meaning; through the mind, as in the faculty of understanding, feeling, desiring, and a way of thinking.[12] The word used in Matthew also occurs twelve other times in the New Testament and tends to render the definition of reflection or contemplation, "thinking through" or "thinking over" an issue. The love we give to God and to others is a love that must be well thought out and contemplated (Ps. 26:2). Loving the Creator and loving His highest creation of man is not merely mindless compliance to the law; it is obedience that is derived from an inward attitude of reflected love (1 Chron. 28:9). The believer is in a relationship with God that ultimately changes his mind, his way of thinking, and his attitude toward God and toward others (Eph. 4:23).

Have you ever been forced to love someone? Well, that is actually an oxymoron. Love, by its very nature must be a choice, not forced. Ok, let me try again, have you ever had to say that you loved someone, but really didn't? When we were little, my brothers and I would pick on each other and we would fight. We were like most siblings; best friends and worst enemies. But the hardest part about fighting was when our mother would make us hug each other, say that we were sorry, and say that we loved each other. I might have been hugging on the outside, but on the inside I was poking their eyes out. I might have been saying "I love you" outwardly, but inwardly I was saying "wait until Momma leaves the room and I'll…" well, I don't have to spell everything out for you. In moments like those, I certainly did not love with thoughtfulness of mind and contemplative determination as the Bible outlines for us.

God will search the minds and the hearts of men (Ps. 7:9) and He will test and know their thoughts (Ps. 139:1, 23). Paul instructs believers to have their minds set on things above and not on things of the earth because their eternal investment is with God, and is not to be set on the temporal matters of this earth (Col. 3:1-4). Unity of the body of believers, in part, is an intellectual endeavor. "If you have any encouragement from being united with Christ, if any comfort from his love, if any fellowship with the Spirit, if any tenderness and compassion, then make my joy

---

[12] James Strong, *The New Strong's Expanded Exhaustive Concordance of the Bible,* "mind," 66.

complete by being like-minded, having the same love, being one in spirit and purpose" (Phil. 2:1-2). God fully expects his followers to train and renew their minds to reflect that of His Son, Jesus (Rom. 12:2). The mind that is not molded to the image of his Son is sinful and hostel toward God (Rom. 8:7). It is the man who trusts and submits his whole being to God that will find rest for his soul and peace for his mind. "You will keep in perfect peace him whose mind is steadfast because he trusts in you. Trust in the Lord forever, for the Lord, the Lord, is the Rock eternal" (Isa. 26:3-4).

Love, as the Bible teaches, is not an emotion or a feeling. It is a well thought out, contemplated decision which involves thinking and acting upon those thoughts. So how does this help you with college? Good question. Remember that it is with the whole of man's being that he is to love God. Man is to love God with the sincerest affections of his heart, with the eternal essence of his soul, with the strength of body and will, and with every thought of his mind. The goal is to endeavor to be fully prepared for college by loving God, loving others and doing so with all our hearts, souls, strength, and **minds**.

Day Two: Time Management

Academics at the high school level can be quite different than at the college level. In high school, you read books (often times together as a class), you take tests (of which your teacher prepared a study guide, and you write papers and essays (five to fifteen page papers or reports). You will do much of the same in college; read, write, and take tests, but on a much more challenging level. Over the next few days we are going to look at some things that I hope will help prepare you to make the most of college and the most out of the wonderful mind that God has given you. Use academics to sharpen your mind so that you can love God and others more perfectly. Grades are not the ultimate goal.

One of the first (and maybe hardest) things to adjust to after high school graduation is a college schedule. There are a number of new factors that you will need to consider while making this transition. New items that you need to add to your schedule may include a part-time or full-time job. Study time will need to be approached a bit differently. Many of your classes were held five days a week while in high school or if you were home-schooled, you or your parents set a schedule according to your needs and their availability. In college, your classes may meet once, twice, or three times a week. Your assignments will need to be scheduled. For every hour you are in class, you need to plan anywhere between three and six hours outside of class preparing for the next session.

You may be assigned a book to read and never talk about it in class, or be asked to write a review on it. You may even begin to think that the professor forgot about the assignment, that is, until you see the semester final! At the beginning of the semester most professors will distribute a syllabus. This is an outline of the class, schedule, tests, and due dates. They may never mention the items on the syllabus again but will fully expect your assignments due on time. College is not like high school where you had someone reminding you to do you homework.

One of the best things you can do to get all of this in, is develop your time management skills. The best thing you can buy yourself is a planner, a calendar, an agenda, a hand held PC, a white board, set of stone tablets, or something on which to write or post your busy schedule and all these new responsibilities.

In budgeting your time, a good place to start is to evaluate what you are doing with your present schedule. Answer the following list of questions to help you decide how much time you presently have to allot to studying and school work.

Evaluation of My Time

1. Average number of hours a day sleeping _____ x 7 = _____
2. Number of hours a day grooming (getting ready) _____ x 7 = _____
3. Number of hours a day eating (including preparation) _____ x 7 = _____
4. Number of hours a day traveling during the week _____ x 5 = _____
5. Number of hours traveled on the weekend _____ x 2 = _____
6. Average number of hours a day in leisure time (TV, reading, sports, hanging out with friends, shopping, music, staring up into the sky etc.) _____ x 7 = _____
7. Average number of hours per day doing errands _____ x 7 = _____
8. Number of hours a week at scheduled gatherings (church, clubs, practice, ministry obligations, tutoring, lessons, meetings etc.) = _____
9. Number of hours a day personal devotion or quiet time _____ x 7 = _____
10. Number of hours a day in class _____ x 5 = _____
11. Number of hours per week working or doing chores = _____

Add the totals = _____

Subtract the total from 168 = _____

This number represents an approximate number of hours you have left in the week to read, study, and do assignments for school. So, the question is…Is this enough time? What can you change in your schedule if this is not enough time to get everything in for school? Could you make better grades with more study time?

The first step in time management is to set goals. This includes long-term, medium-term, and short-term goals. Long-term goals can be as far away as five or ten years. For our purposes, let us think in terms of one semester being the length of our long term goal. Medium-term goals can range over a couple of months to a couple of years. For our purposes let us think in terms of months within the college semester. Short-term goals can be planned for weeks. Again, for our purposes let us think in terms of days and weeks. List some of the academic goals and personal goals that you have at the present time.

Long-term Goals (this semester)

1. _____
2. _____
3. _____
4. _____
5. _____

Medium-term Goals (couple of months)

1. _____
2. _____
3. _____
4. _____
5. _____

Short-term Goals (several days or weeks)

1. _____
2. _____
3. _____
4. _____
5. _____

The next step in managing your time is drawing up a plan to accomplish your goals. I have included a calendar for you to begin charting a plan.

1. Start by listing all the due dates that you know you have and can not change, such as term papers, research papers, book reviews, tests, projects, etc.

2. Estimate how much time you will need to accomplish each goal, then chart it. For example, if you have a comprehensive British Literature test and you know that it will take a minimum of three hours to finish reading the material, four hours to write an essay, and six hours to study for the test, plan to spend an hour a day, thirteen days before the test preparing (start with the reading, then the paper, and finish up with studying material for the test so that the information is fresh on your mind on test day). Or you may want to schedule two hours a day for the week

before your test. Do whatever works best for you. Remember, this is your plan and not every student learns the same way. Use the calendars on the following pages to chart your plan of action for the goals that you listed on page 115.

3. Be open and flexible when it comes to your planning. Life can get crazy and some of the best laid plans may not come to pass. Don't become frustrated, adjust. A pencil (with an eraser) is a good idea when it comes to scheduling.

4. Be sure to note any materials, resources, or assistance you might need to accomplish your goals.

5. Pray through your plan of action and be sure to give thanks to God when you accomplish the goals that He has helped you establish and complete. Celebrate your successes and reward your efforts.

Being Ready

SCHEDULE OF GOALS

MONTH: _____   YEAR: _____

Sun	Mon	Tue	Wed	Thu	Fri	Sat

LIST OF GOALS

_____
_____
_____
_____
_____
_____

A College Preparatory Resource for Third Culture Students

SCHEDULE OF GOALS

MONTH: _____ YEAR: _____

Sun	Mon	Tue	Wed	Thu	Fri	Sat

LIST OF GOALS

_____
_____
_____
_____
_____
_____

Being Ready

SCHEDULE OF GOALS

MONTH: _____   YEAR:

Sun	Mon	Tue	Wed	Thu	Fri	Sat

LIST OF GOALS

_____
_____
_____
_____
_____
_____

A College Preparatory Resource for Third Culture Students

SCHEDULE OF GOALS

MONTH: _____   YEAR:

Sun	Mon	Tue	Wed	Thu	Fri	Sat

LIST OF GOALS

_____
_____
_____
_____
_____
_____

Day Three: Purposeful Reading

I remember thinking that I read a lot in high school. I had no clue what "a lot" was until I got to college. An average to light reading load for a college freshman can reach one hundred pages per week. Like I said earlier, in high school you basically went over the material in the textbook with your teacher. However, in college, the professor expects you to read and understand the text book outside of class. Not many people have ever read a textbook before enrolling in a university course.

Now, there is at least one exception to the above statement...those of you who have home schooled or attended national school during one part of the day and doubled your course load with a US-based curriculum for the rest of the day have a bit of an advantage over the average college student. Many of you have had to read your textbooks, the teacher's text, and additional material because you did not have a teacher to explain it to you. See now, home schooling is not all bad. Having to do the extra reading, having to be resourceful, and basically teaching yourself will prove to be a huge blessing when it comes to your college reading load.

It is important to look at those syllabi (the list of assignments, dues dates, reading etc. that each professor hands out at the beginning for the semester). Write down on a calendar the due dates (goals). Devise a plan of action by scheduling study time, to get all those reading assignments completed. Now that you have a plan of attack, let me offer some suggestions that will help you attack well.

The first thing that you need to determine about the reading assignment is the purpose. Just because you think the professor had nothing better to do than assign you 3,000 pages to read, or because you think he or she is just mean, or because in your paranoia, you think that they are out to get you...is not what I mean by purpose. The purpose will help you decide on a reading strategy. So check out the assignments surrounding the readings. Are you supposed to write an essay evaluating the author's writing and critiquing the ideas in the book? Are you supposed to develop a presentation of practical application? Are you supposed to take a test over the information, answer a series of questions, or be prepared for a class discussion over the material? Each of these requires a different approach.

Reading tips for Evaluation:

1. Find an environment that will allow you to focus on the material (in the game room, at the student center, while driving, or on your bed when you are tired are not good reading environments).

2. Underline items that you agree with and circle the things you don't.

3. Outline the points of argument the author is trying to make.

4. Look for cause and effect in the reading.

5. Write questions that challenge the writer's point of view or develop an opposing argument.

Reading tips for Practical Application:

1. Again reading environment is important. Being in front of the TV is a bad idea, so is playing games on the computer.

2. Determine the specific goal for the material begin read.

3. Place post-it notes in the sections that meet the specific goal. If there is more than one goal, use various colors of post-it notes or highlighters; a different color for each goal.

4. Make a list, as you read, of items that you have learned, points that you can use, or new ideas that you have learned.

5. After you have read, noted, and listed, then write out how and where you can use each point of new information.

Being Ready

Reading tips for Understanding:

1. Have I mentioned how important your environment is while reading?

2. Determine the general outline of the reading. Bold print, italicized writing, and section headings help out a lot with outlining.

3. Underline the specific facts that support the general outline of the reading (be careful not to underline everything. Judge for yourself what is the absolute most important point and then underline only the key words (the subject of the sentence, objects, direct objects, and verbs are most often key words).

4. Be sure to know if there is something specific the professor wants to find in the reading (answers to a list of questions, determine the most important point, what was the sequence of events etc.) before you start to read.

5. Summarize the general ideas and the specific points, If there is space, do so in the margin of the book (as long as you own the book, that is).

Read the head line in your local or national news paper. You will be reading for understanding. After you read the article you will be asked to outline the general sequence of the information, describe the characters, and state the main point of the essay.

1. Secure a quiet reading environment.

2. As you read, look for the purpose of the book according to the essay.

3. Then, as you read, underline important facts (names, events, lessons).

4. In the margin of the page, write general headings for each paragraph.

5. Summarize the essay in a simple outline.

Article Outline

Being Ready

A College Preparatory Resource for Third Culture Students

Day Four: Taking Note of Things

Another one of those not so subtle differences between high school and college is taking lecture notes. Until I went to college, I had not even taken note of my grocery list, much less notes in class. I remember the first day of my freshman year of college, sitting in my Western Civilization class enjoying the great "story" the professor was sharing. Then a classmate leaned over and asked me if I got the date of something the professor had said in my notes. All I could remember thinking was…notes?...what notes? In college, taking lecture notes is fundamental. I would like to share with you some pearls of wisdom that I have gained since my freshman year of college.

Why Take Notes?: If you are going to develop a habit of doing something, it is important to know why and if it is beneficial. If you were venturing a guess, why would you think note-taking during a lecture, would be helpful? List your ideas.

_____
_____
_____
_____
_____
_____
_____
_____
_____
_____
_____
_____
_____
_____
_____
_____

Being Ready

Did you include in the list that note-taking provides material from which to study for tests and write papers, much of the test material may not be covered in the text, helps you listen better, it will involve you more in class discussion, organizes your thoughts, notes give you something to work with later in processing hard to understand class information, develops critical thinking skills that are needed in most every career. Besides, it makes you look smart.

Note Taking Methods: This is not a comprehensive list. The truth is there are as many note taking methods as there are students taking notes. These are three methods that work well for me. Find what works best for you and what works best for the type of lecture (and lecturer) that you have in class.

- **Chronological Method of Note Taking-** With this method, you basically are taking notes in the order that the professor is giving the information. Most often, if the information pertains to systems, patterns, or historical events, your professor will present the material in sequential order. If dates or steps are presented out of order, when you revise your notes your can rewrite the information in the correct order. Here is an example.

```
Western Civilization 101
        9/18/0000
    I. 1842 - xxxx happened first
            - because of this yyyy went
to xxxx
            - xxxx resulted

    II. 1845 - zzzz was the first to zzzz
            - xxxx, xxxx, xxxx, and xxxx
```

Topical Method of Note Taking- With this method, you are basically grouping together the various subjects into like categories. Once you identify that the professor is lecturing on a subject matter that has groupings of common elements, and then separate the groups by symbols. When you rewrite and refine your notes, you can put the items together. But while you are in class, just note the difference in the margin. The following will give you an idea of what I am talking about.

	Western Civilization 101
	9/18/xxxx
○	▲I. 1842- xxxx first happened
	▶■ - because
of this yyyy went to xxxx	
	●II. 1845 – zzzz was the first to
zzzz	
	▲ xxxx, xxxx, xxxx, and xxxx

As you are taking notes, you can group the information, quickly and easily. When you rewrite and refine the information, all you have to do is gather all the ▲ pieces of information together, all the ■ pieces of information together, and all the ● pieces of information together. Notice how, in the second line, I made the triangle at a ninety degree turn (▶■) that is to remind me that this line of information will be written in two different groupings when I rewrite and refine my notes.

- **Mapping Method of Taking Notes-** I find that this method works particularly well when I can not pick up on the professor's cues, patterns, or method of delivering information. Instructors who are "rabbit chasers" are often hard to follow with notes. This method is a lot like brainstorming where you write down all the random pieces of information then try connecting it with a series of diagrams.

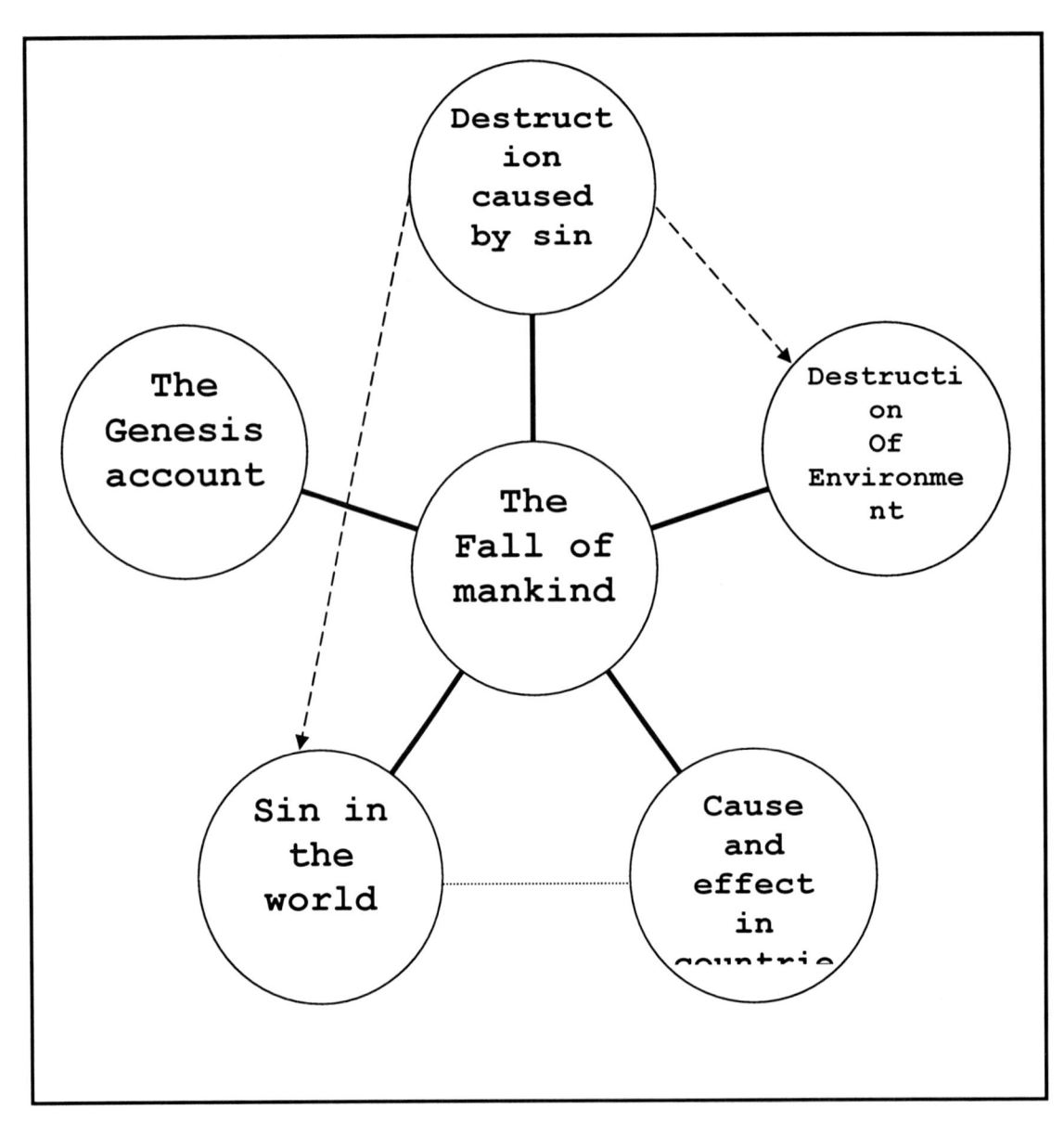

```
                    Destruction
                    caused
                    by sin

   The                                    Destruction
   Genesis                                Of
   account          The                   Environment
                    Fall of
                    mankind

       Sin in               Cause
       the                  and
       world                effect
                            in
                            countries
```

Note Taking Tips: The following are ideas to help the note taking process work for you. Regardless of what method you choose, these ten items are designed to make the most out of your efforts.

1. Read the text information before class. If you will be discussing a subject that you are not familiar with, do a little research for definitions and basic information that would help you understand the lecture.
2. Stay focused and keep it simple. Use symbols, not elaborate art work (not counting the doodling).

3. Keep it consistent. If you use color to code your notes, stick with the same colors for the same items.
4. Review your notes as soon after class as possible. Check for incorrect information and missing information.
5. Rewrite or reorganize your notes into manageable clusters of information.
6. Title, label, and date your notes while you are in class.
7. Review and study your class notes before tests and quizzes.
8. Use your notes to make practice questions and flash cards for test preparation.
9. When it is possible, use the main points of class notes for research paper or presentation resource (you will need to cite the information from a lecturer. Check your writer's manual to know how this is done).
10. Summarize the information. Do not write word for word what the speaker is saying (writer's cramp will overtake you). Look for key word (subject, verbs, direct and indirect objects of a sentence). Keep it short and concise, but do not leave out the important stuff. For example do not write; "waged war." Who declared war on whom? Instead write; "CR war → GR" (that is, if you can remember what CR and GR stands for)."

Note Taking Assignment: Watch or listen to the News, decide a method, and take notes. Choose the lead story (do not read about it). Practice your listening.

News Notes

_____
_____
_____
_____
_____
_____
_____
_____
_____
_____

Being Ready

Day Five: Research and Writing

University level academics most often encompass three basic learning skills; reading, test taking, and writing. There is the occasional project or presentation, but the three biggies are these. We have looked at reading and note taking (which are big factors in being ready for tests). We are going to finish our study with some thoughts on research and writing.

Thoughts on Library Research: Pay close attention during your new student orientation. That giant building in the center of the campus is important. It is called the library. That is where they stick all those things called books. I know that many of you are accustomed to doing most of your research via the internet; especially if you grew up in the outer edges of the bush, in small villages, or in a small international or MK school. The internet has been a huge blessing to the world of education. While the internet is amazing, books still have a lot to offer our knowledge base.

Become familiar with your university's cataloguing system. Most US colleges use the Dewy Decimal system. A tour of the library is normally offered during your orientation week. If it is not offered, then make an appointment with the librarian to get someone to show you how the system works. You will make their day by being interested in the library. Since the advent of the internet I am sure many librarians have suffered from student neglect, or a deficit of student interest in the library. They will be pleased and surprised that you are asking for help.

Most libraries will have a front desk and someone there to help you with your questions and to check-in and check-out books, but very few schools have the labor force to have people standing by to locate books for people who do not know how to use the library, so become familiar with your university's library.

A general layout of the library would include the *reference area* (encyclopedias, dictionaries, almanacs, atlases, doctoral dissertations and project), the *stacks* (this is the fun name for all of the books, magazines, and journals found in the library), the *periodicals area* (scholarly magazines and journals and in this area along with newspapers), *audio/visual area* (you will find art, audio recordings, and media items here. Check out this area. Most libraries have these huge CDs called record albums which are played on special equipment call record players…they are really cool), *computer area* (most of these terminals are linked to the internet and to the data base of the library. This way you can type in a book or topic that you are researching and the onscreen information should tell you where to find it. For our purposes here, we are not going to get into how to find books because not every school uses the same system). The last area most libraries will have is the **microform area** (microforms are materials printed that have been reduced in size and copied on small films called microfilm or microfiche. These films require particular equipment to view the information so your school might have a set-aside reading room for this material).

A few other things that is great about libraries:

- Full of information (not just a good place to nap in between classes).
- There is a wonderful feeling of being surrounded by great intellect as you walk through the stacks.
- It looks impressive when you walk out of there with ten or fifteen books in your arms for a research paper.
- In regard to the last one, you will not have to do as many reps at the gym.
- The internet is great but there is nothing like the feel of a book (just don't write in them! Librarians hate that).
- Books are easier to transport to the park or beach, than is the computer.

Thoughts on Research Writing: The types of writing you may encounter at the university level are; research papers, essays, reports, critical evaluations, and summaries. Nearly all of your general courses will require one or more of these types of assignments. Because each professor may require something different, we will not summarize your high school English class, with a review of how to write a research paper. I listed some thoughts that might help as you approach your assignments.

- Start early. As soon as you know what the assignment and topic are, begin to schedule research and writing time (it is nearly impossible to write a good research paper twenty-four hours before it is due).
- Use a variety of resources such as books, journals, newspapers, media, and references, not just a variety of internet sites.
- Use the most up-to-date resources available.

- Read as many authors as possible pertaining to your subject. Summarize what they have to say, about your topic, then group that information into sections or subheadings for your paper.
- Take notes while you are researching and don't forget to record the bibliography information (title and subtitle of the resource, authors or editors, publishing location – city, state, and country, publishing company, date of publication, and the page numbers where you gained that information.
- If you write down a direct quote from an author be sure to put it in quotation marks. Be sure to record the information correctly.
- ALWAYS, ALWAYS, ALWAYS cite your information ALWAYS!!!!!
- Type your papers, black ink and unless otherwise stated by your professor. Use one inch margins, double space, and twelve point "Times New Roman" font. (Make it neat, don't use your paper as a coffee coaster or stuff in the bottom of your backpack).
- Use a writer's manual to know how to set up your paper. Check to see if your university requires a certain writing style.
- EDIT: read your work out loud and have someone else read it.

The Study at a Glance

✝

Objectives

To learn from other MKs and TCKs who are transitioning to college in the United States

To summarize what was learned during the study

To evaluate the course and explore ways to improve the course for future groups

✝

Verse

"Like Your name, O God Your praise reaches to the ends of the earth; your right hand is filled with righteousness."
　　-Psalm 48:10

✝

"For this God is our God for ever and ever; He will be our guide even to the end."
　　-Psalm 48:14

Unit Seven: Closing Thoughts

I can not take credit for this project alone. Many people were involved in making it happen. Before we finish up our study, I want to introduce you to these wonderful people and I want to thank them for helping me see this project through and for helping me learn and grow as I researched and wrote.

To my instructors Gary, Johnny, Jo, Judy and Bill; thank you for your leadership and guidance. To the curriculum team; Tina, Kay, and Cheryl, thank you for your editing, your input, and your encouragement. To Stefanie and Julie thank you for your constant friendship, encouragement, prayers, and for correcting my US American "vernacular." To the teachers and students of Sojourn Academy, Costa Rica, and to the teachers and students of Mexico City Christian Academy, Mexico, you are my inspiration!

Gracias

What Others Have Experienced

God has given me the really cool privilege of working with some great students over the years. I graduated from college in May of 1990 and was in Costa Rica working with MKs and TCKs in August of 1990. This has been my constant ministry ever since. I have asked some of my former students to pass on their thoughts to you. The following are their responses, to my questions, as they wrote them.

MK Responses to Survey Questions

What was the hardest thing about transitioning to your college?

1. The size of the school and the size of the classroom took some getting used to. Also being back in the states to live and not just as a vacation was a little hard to adjust to.

2. I found that I had a poor background in World History. It's one of my weak points and it was not taught to me in El Salvador, where my family was till they went to Mexico.

3. Not knowing the culture, not having my family there my first semester to help me get established/set up. I was in a new state, so I had no friends to go to, but made some soon off the bat, but it was hard at first to try and go out and meet people (now, no worries at all).

4. Being alone and with people who you thought had nothing in common with you and didn't care to hear about your life.

5. I really missed Suriname and the close knit community there... Also the difference between doing independent study high school and having to go to classes and deal with professors at Georgetown.

6. Getting used to waking up early after the summer, finding a good church, finding things to do on the weekends.

7. The hardest thing about transitioning to college was being so far away from my family. It was also extremely hard to not have a church or missionary family around me when I was first getting settled into my life here in Chicago.

8. Choosing a major without knowing exactly how I am to use it afterwards. I was a Bio major and switched to English as the Lord began to teach me more of the talents He has given me and the ways in which He can use me because of those talents. I had a very hard time choosing a major because I was uncertain of how to decide on a career plan, what I should base that decision on and how to critically evaluate the MANY options.

9. Learning how to study was definitely a difficult challenge for me. The amount of course content for each class was overwhelming and there was almost no time to learn it.

10. Haven't yet, but will probably be being in an environment where I have to fend for myself (aka independence), but spiritually also.

11. Getting used to the busy schedule, being on time for classes, and getting used to my roommate.

12. The hardest part about college was realizing that I couldn't get my parents to solve all of my problems anymore. I had to take the initiative and get things done such as bills, insurance, etc. Also, I couldn't talk to my parents anytime I wanted to or go home when I wanted a break.

13. I think the hardest part was not being able to speak my 2nd language to other people. Sometimes I like to express myself in another language besides English and all of the sudden, no one else understood this other language I spoke.

What do you wish you would have known before going to college?

1. Being in college is expensive and it's VERY important to learn how to manage your money and your time.

2. As I said, class-wise, World History. And I wish I had known about the economy of the USA and how completely screwed-up and complicated it is.

3. That people in the U.S. are very closed minded when it comes to trying to accept others from different backgrounds, I think I would have been a bit more cautious when I told people I was from another country before they judged me as an outsider.

4. I can't expect everyone else to change, I am the one who had learned to be flexible so I needed to adapt to them, not hate them for not understanding.

5. I wish I could've known more about what it would actually be like~ I had absolutely no idea what to expect...

6. How to cook.

7. It would have been nice to have had some time to learn to drive and get my drivers' license, as well as understand more thoroughly how the U.S. government (on a local and country-wide level) works. I also wish that I had known more about the colleges that tend to have a larger MK population.

8. That undergrad is not such a final decision. My master's degree will carry more importance and therefore, I can major in any field I enjoy and choose to focus on. I wish I'd known that if I choose to go on to graduate school, which allows for me to define my career better.

9. I wish I had a better understanding of how our brains process information, so I could study more effectively. Perhaps a book or a psychology course would have sufficed.(but I eventually learnt through a book!).

10. I will find out soon enough.

11. That it isn't as rough or depressing as I thought it would be, so I had no need to be as stressed out as I was. It would've been Far better to rest in God.

12. I wish I would have known that college is not always the "best time of your life". Although it was wonderful, it has its ups and downs just like any other part of life.

13. I wish I would have known more about what American expect of you. For example, in Mexico if you're late to a meeting nobody thinks anything about it, but here it's different. It's hard to explain how they feel, but I wish I would have known more about their feelings about certain situations, like lateness.

What would have helped you make the transition easier?

1. Something that really helped make the transition easier was having my parents in the states with me. They were furloughing in Oklahoma, so I could go to their house for dinner or for the afternoon. They were going through some of the same culture shock as I was and so I had them to depend on.

2. Better background in how the "system" works. It's hard trying to get things done in the right way without some financial business on your rear all the time. Some of my classes are easy and I get by alright but overall it is rather difficult.

3. Spending maybe a couple of months here before I was thrown out into the world of the U.S. Maybe I would have picked some things up culturally, learned some of the modern dialect, just little things that would have helped me get a heads up on people so I would know what was going on. I hope it helps; I am not sure those answers were what you were looking for. Hope things are going well for you.

4. I don't think that any big transition is ever easy, I am not sure, I guess you just have to live through it to learn about life and get stronger and learn more about your self.

5. Maybe if I had gone to some kind of summer college prep program in the States I wouldn't have had such a rough transition. I think part of the problem was that I'd never really gone to a regular school in the States so when I started at Georgetown, I was even more culture shocked than the other freshmen...

6. A better knowledge of the area around the college.

7. The transition might have been easier if my family had been in the area during at least my first several weeks of college. It also may have been easier if there had been a group of MKs here on campus that I could have been informed of and gotten locked into for support and encouragement during the transition time. I think the most important element of my being able to transition well was, along with branching out, staying in close contact with my nuclear and missionary family, especially my MK cousins from my home in Mexico.

8. I would have been less frustrated and more decisive on a certain major. Had I known someone who could explain to me my different options and opened my eyes to the opportunities and my abilities and the best ways to use those. I felt like every counselor I spoke with expected me to already know what I wanted to do and that I had a clear idea of all the possible careers---I have learned of new careers lately that I wish I'd known about earlier on in my college career. They treated me as though I really knew what I wanted and what I was talking about. I didn't really "believe" in counselors. It would have been useful to have maximized their tools and advice.

9. A PRACTICE RUN! haha. Before going to Queen's University, we had various orientations which were somewhat helpful. We discussed concerns with upper year students and throughout the orientation they would give us their thoughts, tips, and lessons learned... anything from best study locations to time management skills.

10. Most likely having friends or people that I already know at the college/university.

11. Visiting the college, and especially sitting in on a few classes.

12. First it would have helped if I had some sort of adopted family in the town where I went to college, I had this the last year and I enjoyed it very much. Also second, and I know this sounds weird, but I wish I would have had Instant Messenger when I started college, b/c can't call of your friends that live over seas and I think it would have helped me keep in touch with them better.

13. When I got here and needed money, I thought it would be easier to just get a job, impress the people and "work my way up" really quickly. It was a much slower process. I think it would have helped if someone would have explained to me more about jobs, interviews, resumes, and stuff like that.

Being Ready

1. What comments stood out to you?

2. What kind of wisdom can you glean from these college students?

3. In preparing for college, what might you do differently or take in to consideration after reading these comments?

A College Preparatory Resource for Third Culture Students

Summary Time

Here we are at the end of our study together. Wow, it seems like time has flown by! We have covered a lot of ground and have looked at a lot of material. When we take in large amounts of information, spend a good amount of energy evaluating our lives, and planning for our futures, it is a good idea to stop and review the things that God has taught us along the way. We do not want to miss any important lessons. Take some time to go back over the units of lessons, summarizing each. Note what was helpful and what was not so relevant to you at this time. Then conclude by writing down at least one thing that God taught you, reminded you of, revealed to you, or impressed upon you for each unit.

Unit One: Our Relationship with God

1. Summarize the week by listing the main points of the unit.

2. Write what was most helpful to you.

3. Write what was least helpful to you.

4. What did God teach you (or is still teaching you) through this unit's study?

Unit Two: Our Relationship with Others

1. Summarize the week by listing the main points of the unit.

2. Write what was most helpful to you.

3. Write what was least helpful to you.

4. What did God teach you (or is still teaching you) through this unit's study?

Unit Three: Loving with the Heart – Emotional Preparation

1. Summarize the week by listing the main points of the unit.

_____
_____
_____
_____
_____
_____
_____

2. Write what was most helpful to you.

_____
_____
_____
_____

3. Write what was least helpful to you.

_____
_____
_____
_____

4. What did God teach you (or is still teaching you) through this unit's study?

_____
_____
_____
_____
_____
_____
_____

A College Preparatory Resource for Third Culture Students

Unit Four: Loving with the Soul – Spiritual Preparation

1. Summarize the week by listing the main points of the unit.

2. Write what was most helpful to you.

3. Write what was least helpful to you.

4. What did God teach you (or is still teaching you) through this unit's study?

Unit Five: Loving with Strength – Physical Preparation

1. Summarize the week by listing the main points of the unit.

_____
_____
_____
_____
_____
_____
_____

2. Write what was most helpful to you.

_____
_____
_____

3. Write what was least helpful to you.

_____
_____
_____

4. What did God teach you (or is still teaching you) through this unit's study?

_____
_____
_____
_____
_____
_____
_____

Unit Six: Loving with the Mind – Intellectual Preparation

1. Summarize the week by listing the main points of the unit.

2. Write what was most helpful to you.

3. Write what was least helpful to you.

4. What did God teach you (or is still teaching you) through this unit's study?

Class Evaluation

If you have used this material as a part of a class it might be helpful to you and to your leader to evaluation the class. Please answer the following questions to the best of your ability. Feel free to expound upon any of your answers.

1. Do you feel that the workbook was clear and easy to understand? If not, please tell me what parts were not clear or easy to understand.

   _____
   _____
   _____
   _____
   _____

2. Do you feel the topics we looked at will help you in being ready for college? If not, please explain?

   _____
   _____
   _____
   _____
   _____

3. What would you leave out of this class and workbook? Why?

   _____
   _____
   _____
   _____
   _____
   _____

4. What would you add to this class and or workbook? Why?

_____
_____
_____
_____
_____
_____
_____
_____
_____
_____
_____
_____
_____

5. Do you feel this class will be helpful to other students? Why or why not?

_____
_____
_____
_____
_____

6. What did you like the most about the class?

_____
_____
_____
_____
_____
_____

7. What did you like the least about the class?

_____
_____
_____
_____
_____
_____

Please circle the answer that best describes your impression:

1 strongly disagree, 2 disagree, 3 did not observe, 4 agree, or 5 highly agree

1. The leader clearly presented the learning objectives for each unit.
    1   2   3   4   5

2. I felt that the leader placed proper emphasis on the spiritual and Biblical importance of preparing for college.
    1   2   3   4   5

3. I believe the leader understood of the need students to be prepared for college.
    1   2   3   4   5

4. I felt the leader effectively taught each unit.
    1   2   3   4   5

5. I rank the leader's overall direction as:
    1   2   3   4   5

References

Books

Pascarella, Ernest T. and Patrick T. Terenzini. *How College Affects Students.* San Francisco: Jossey-Bass Publishers, 1991.

Smith, Christian and Melinda Lundquist Denton. *Soul Searching: The Religious and Spiritual Lives of American Teenagers.* Oxford: Oxford University Press, 2005.

Strong, James. *The New Strong's Expanded Exhaustive Concordance of the Bible.* Nashville: Thomas Nelson Publishers, 2001.

Internet Sites

Barna, George. *Church Demographics.* Ventura: The Barna Group, 2005 [on-line]. Accessed 4 January 2005. Available from www.barna.org; Internet.

Barna, George. *Family.* Ventura: The Barna Group, 2005 [on-line]. Accessed 4 January 2005. Available from www.barna.org; Internet.

International Mission Board. *Historical Reflection.* Richmond: International Mission Board, 2005 [on-line]. Accessed 8 June 2005. Available from www.imb.org; Internet.

National Heart, Lung, and Blood Institute "For Parents: Why Sleep is So Important." *Star Sleeper.* Bethesda: National Heart, Lung, and Blood Institute, 2006 [on-line]. Accessed 18 February 2006. Available from www.nhlbi.nih.gov/health/public/sleep/starslp/parents/whysleep.htm; Internet.

US Department of Agriculture. *My Pyramid: Steps to a Healthier You.* Alexandria: US Department of Agriculture, 2006 [on-line]. Accessed 18 February 2006. Available from www.mypyramid.gov; Internet.

US Department of Health and Human Services: Administration for Children and Families. *Children and Families Glossary.* Washington DC: US Department of Health and Human Services, 2005 [on-line]. Accessed 5 May 2005. Available from www.hhs.gov; Internet.

Staggs, Brandon. *King James Dictionary*, "soul." Gdansk: StudyLight, 2005 [on-line]. Accessed 12 September 2005. Available from www.studylight.com; Internet.

Interviews

Price, Carolyn, associate of The Global Research Information Center. Interviewed by author, 21 June 2005, Richmond. Electronic correspondence. International Mission Board, Richmond.

Speeches

Derouen, Johnny, American *Families in Crises Research.* Class lecture for Human Growth and Development, [March 21, 2005]. Southwestern Baptist Theological Seminary, Ft. Worth, Texas.

Jones Ian F. "The Question and the Call, Chapel October 27, 2004." Fort Worth: Southwestern Baptist Theological Seminary, 2004. Speech.